Smell and the Past

Smell and the Past

Noses, Archives, Narratives

William Tullett

BLOOMSBURY ACADEMIC
LONDON • NEW YORK • OXFORD • NEW DELHI • SYDNEY

BLOOMSBURY ACADEMIC
Bloomsbury Publishing Plc
50 Bedford Square, London, WC1B 3DP, UK
1385 Broadway, New York, NY 10018, USA
29 Earlsfort Terrace, Dublin 2, Ireland

BLOOMSBURY, BLOOMSBURY ACADEMIC and the Diana logo
are trademarks of Bloomsbury Publishing Plc

First published in Great Britain 2023
This paperback edition published in 2024

Copyright © William Tullett, 2023

William Tullett has asserted his right under the Copyright,
Designs and Patents Act, 1988, to be identified as Author of this work.

For legal purposes the Acknowledgements on pp. ix–x constitute
an extension of this copyright page.

Cover image © Deutsches Spionagemuseum. www.deutsches-spionagemuseum.de

This work is published open access subject to a Creative Commons Attribution-NonCommercial-NoDerivatives 4.0 International licence (CC BY-NC-ND 4.0, https://creativecommons.org/licenses/by-nc-nd/4.0/). You may re-use, distribute, and reproduce this work in any medium for non-commercial purposes, provided you give attribution to the copyright holder and the publisher and provide a link to the Creative Commons licence.

Bloomsbury Publishing Plc does not have any control over, or responsibility for, any third-party websites referred to or in this book. All internet addresses given in this book were correct at the time of going to press. The author and publisher regret any inconvenience caused if addresses have changed or sites have ceased to exist, but can accept no responsibility for any such changes.

A catalogue record for this book is available from the British Library

A catalog record for this book is available from the Library of Congress

ISBN: HB: 978-1-3503-6752-4
PB: 978-1-3503-6755-5
ePDF: 978-1-3503-6753-1
eBook: 978-1-3503-6754-8

Typeset by Integra Software Services Pvt. Ltd.

To find out more about our authors and books visit www.bloomsbury.com
and sign up for our newsletters.

For Hugo and Milo, two discerning noses, and my Odeuropa colleagues.

Contents

List of figures	viii
Acknowledgements	ix
Introduction: On being nose-wise	1
1 Noses	13
The stench of books and trees	17
Archival absences	23
Material presences and olfactory affordances	28
Re-odorizing the material archive	35
Making politics sensible	40
Epistemicides	42
2 Archives	45
Falstaff's nose	47
Volatile records	57
Sniffing around	66
3 Narratives	75
The scent of time	77
The temporality of scent-less-ness	81
The archaeology of an odour	88
Beyond see-what-you-smell	94
Of 'notes', 'narratives' and presences	106
Conclusion: Nose-first	117
Bibliography	122
Index	141

Figures

Olfactory Figures

At various points in this book you will be asked to sniff common materials that evoke the scent of the past because of the shared molecules and compounds that give both past and contemporary materials their particular odour. Below you can find a list of these Olfactory Figures, with a few suggested materials for each example. This book can be read without these figures, but the argument of the book depends on encouraging the reader to engage their nose and so they are essential to the full experience of engaging with this text.

OF 0.1	Breathe in your surroundings. Give your immediate environment a good sniff – both the ambient atmosphere and the objects around you. Does the space where you are reading this have a particular smell? How has this impacted your reading of this text so far?	11
OF 1.1	Sniff the ammonia in stale urine (human, cat) or smelling salts	24
OF 1.2	Sniff truffles or, more likely, truffle oil	30
OF 1.3	Light a safety match, blow it out and sniff the smoke	32
OF 2.1	This book and any other number of books you have around you (try, if you can, to sniff of varying vintages and materials)	67
OF 2.2	Root beer and some – especially in the UK – rubs and sprays for muscle pain from high street chemists	71
OF 2.3	Saffron threads – the sort you might find in a supermarket	73
OF 3.1	As you read this chapter, you could, if you so choose, burn a stick of incense	75
OF 3.2	Bleaching powder or liquid bleach (the active ingredient of which is chloride of lime). Just a quick sniff …	85
OF 3.3	Dried or fresh rosemary, rubbing it between your fingers to help release the scent	95
OF 3.4	Benzoin resin, incense or gum	108

Acknowledgements

This book could not have happened without my colleagues on the EU Horizon 2020 funded 'Odeuropa' project. Working with them has utterly transformed my perspective on smell and how we study it. Special thanks go to Inger Leemans, the project's leader, whose generosity and support, intellectual curiosity and determination have provided so much inspiration. I would like to thank Inger, Melanie Kiechle, Lizzie Marx, Jan Van Dijkhuizen and an anonymous reviewer who read and offered extensive comments on the draft of the book. Alex Wragge-Morley deserves special mention as a sounding board, dealing both generously and in good humour with my worries that the pandemic had driven me to write a book that made no sense to anybody including myself. I have presented this material and gained useful feedback from seminars at Anglia Ruskin University, the University of Cambridge, the IIAS in Jerusalem, Durham University and Lancaster University. My thanks go to all of those who attended these talks and gave invaluable comments and suggestions. My now wife, Natasha, already has all of my love but deserves all of my thanks as well for her support and encouragement. Hugo and Milo, our cats, have often forced me to step away from the laptop (by sitting on it) and thereby encouraged me to think through my ideas at a little more length.

However, this book also draws on an extensive interdisciplinary scholarship on smell. Academic culture, which sometimes prizes innovation over understanding, often forces scholars to claim an originality for their work that belies the pre-existing panoply of publications both in their own discipline and outside it. One of the great joys of the 'Odeuropa' project with which I am involved has been bringing together scholars that I admire and getting to work collaboratively alongside them. Those who wish to delve into this fantastic scholarship can consult the bibliography at the end of this book. But they would do even better to examine the online bibliography that can be found at https://www.zotero.org/groups/4530561/pastscent/library. This list, with over 700 entries and counting, demonstrates that the book you are reading is just one part of an extensive, ongoing, scholarly discussion about smell. I hope that after tackling the ideas contained in these pages, you will be inspired to contribute your voice and your nose to that conversation.

Introduction: On being nose-wise

In his novel *The Sense of the Past*, Henry James tells the story of a historian, named Ralph Pendrel, for whom mere words and texts could never be enough to capture the feeling of the past. What Pendrel wanted was:

> the very smell of that simpler mixture of things that had so long served; he wanted the very tick of the old stopped clocks ... He wanted the unimaginable accidents, the little notes of truth for which the common lens of history, however the scowling muse might bury her nose, was not sufficiently fine. He wanted evidence of a sort for which there had never been documents enough or for which documents mainly, however, multiplied, would never be enough.[1]

What if we were actually able to smell out the mixture of things that composed the olfactory past? What if historians were to bury their noses in the past instead of merely resorting to ocular inspection?

This short book provides some answers to these questions. It is an exploration of what it means to study smell *in* the past, smell *and* the past and the smell *of* the past.

These are three quite distinct things.

Smell *in* the past refers to the shifting smellscapes of past societies and how people understood, categorized and responded to odours. In other words, smell *in* the past refers to the social and cultural role of scents and their sensing. Disinterring smell in the past relies on close and careful *reading* of texts and images. This is the kind of approach characteristic of much of the work published by humanities scholars on the sensory past. It is deeply influenced by anthropology, one of the fields that has been at the forefront of

---

[1] Henry James, *The Sense of the Past* (New York: W. Collins Sons & Co., 1917), pp. 49–50.

sensory studies, and cultural history. This approach holds that smell is deeply cultural, and both contemporary and historical responses to odours have always been informed by perceptual lenses that have been specific to a period, place or community. For instance, whilst Renaissance writers emphasized the scent of the rose and gave it great symbolic importance, shifting modes of perception in the nineteenth century led gardeners breeding roses to select for visual beauty rather than fragrance.[2] Excavating these lenses involves an attunement to textual evidence and a recognition that smells – and noses – are in the past, historians are in the present, and that the gulf of historical distance means the two cannot (or indeed should not) meet.[3] This historical distance, which has long been a mythic feature of the way historians define themselves, is also what frustrates Pendrel and leads him to fantasize about a more immediate way of accessing past experience (a fantasy that comes true when he time-travels back to 1820s London).[4]

But this is not the only way to think about the relationship between smells and the past. In this book smell *and* the past refers to the role history plays in memory, heritage and public history: smell and our sense of 'past-ness'.[5] Smell, as for Pendrel, is sometimes offered as a route to 'immersive' pasts (a role that invites both celebration and suspicion).[6] Thinking about smell *and* the past means asking why and how this connection developed, and what it means for our understanding of smell's relationship with society and culture both today and in the future. For a historical example we could turn to Carole Rawcliffe's work, which has explored how Victorian sanitarians constructed a view of medieval towns and cities – as stinking cesspits mired in filth – which remains influential today despite being at odds with what archival research tells us.[7] We

---

[2] Constance Classen, *Worlds of Sense: Exploring the Senses in History and across Cultures* (London: Routledge, 1993), pp. 15–36.

[3] Mark Smith, *Sensing the Past: Seeing, Hearing, Smelling, Tasting, and Touching History* (Berkeley: University of California Press, 2007), p. 5; Rob Boddice and Mark Smith, *Emotions, Senses, Experience* (Cambridge: Cambridge University Press, 2020), p. 23.

[4] See Mark Salber Phillips, *On Historical Distance* (London: Yale University Press, 2013).

[5] This is a subject of much discussion in heritage; see for example Cornelius Holtorf, 'The Presence of Pastness: Themed Environments and Beyond', in Carolyn Oesterle et al. (eds.), *Staging the Past: Themed Environments in Transcultural Perspective* (Bielefeld: Transcript Verlag, 2014), pp. 23–40.

[6] See the chapters by Richard J. Stevenson, Andreas Keller and Jim Drobnick in Nina Levent and Alvaro-Pascual-Leone (eds.), *The Multisensory Museum: Cross-Disciplinary Perspectives on Touch, Sound, Smell, Memory, and Space* (Lanham, MA: Rowman and Littlefield, 2014).

[7] Carole Rawcliffe, *Urban Bodies: Communal Health in Late Medieval English Towns and Cities* (Woodbridge: Boydell and Brewer, 2013), pp. 12–24.

must go further than the oft-repeated point about contemporary experiences of smell being different – in sensitivities to scent, in the meanings given to odours and in the way individuals conceptualize olfactory experience – to historical ones. We can explore how and why those experiences are different to those that existed in the past and be open to the possibility of finding continuities as well as change in how people sniffed. Such explorations will allow us to explore difference alongside the historical residues of sensation and bodily habits that still inform the way we sense the past, our present and our futures today.

Finally, we should distinguish these first two from the smell *of* the past. This refers to the smells that might have materially existed at any one point in the past and whose remains we can detect or, through a careful mix of historical sources and material literacy, imagine today. The smell *of* the past is a story of volatile organic compounds (VOCs) and the molecules that make up scents. It is a story for which documents may 'never be enough', but for which material and sensuous evidence is vital. This is a story that would involve a different history altogether: tracing, as the food-writer Harold McGee has suggestively intimated, a molecular history of odours over time.[8] It is also a story with a different relationship to the archive. As Anna Chen has persuasively argued, smells can be archived in the traditional sense in institutional repositories and collections. Odours can be bottled and they can be stored with audio or textual descriptions of the meanings and feelings they evoke. However, smells are also archives in miniature: they are repositories of memories and feeling.[9] What is more, materialities beyond the traditional archive can inform our olfactory histories. Bodies can act as repositories for long-sedimented attitudes to odours. Objects can possess residues of the odours with which they have come into contact. Architectural spaces and their flows of air can reveal how scent might have moved within a space. All of these elements of the wider archive can contribute to a history that traces odorous material accretions in spaces and on objects through both human and machine-mediated sniffing.[10] This is

---

[8] Harold McGee, *Nose-Dive: A Field Guide to the World's Smells* (London: John Murray, 2020).
[9] Anna Chen, 'Perfume and Vinegar: Olfactory Knowledge, Remembrance, and Recordkeeping', *The American Archivist*, 79:1 (2016), pp. 103–20.
[10] For an example of this work, see Cecilia Bembibre and Matija Strlič, 'Smell of Heritage: A Framework for the Identification, Analysis and Archival of Historic Odours', *Heritage Science*, 5 (2017), p. 2.

a history that recognizes and makes productive use of the fungible, decaying and ever-shifting nature of archives.[11]

When combined together, these three approaches offer a way of understanding smell that is not just about meaning, the main bill of fare for humanities scholars, but also the material affordances that environments today and in the past can provide for exploring 'presence' – understood as the 'phenomena and conditions that contribute to the production of meaning, without being meaning themselves'.[12]

To give a personal example, I recently attended a workshop held at the Sam Wanamaker theatre in London, a space created as an ideal-type representation of a seventeenth-century indoor London theatre.[13] The workshop was organized by the *Atmospheric Theatre* project, which has explored the relationship between theatre spaces, performance and the awareness of air quality and pollution. Led by Chloe Preedy and Freya Verlander, the workshop involved actors performing scenes from seventeenth-century plays whilst deploying the scents – ranging from incense and balsam to rosemary, lavender and lilies – that were included in the original stage directions.[14]

Despite the air-management unit, which is required to enable the use of beeswax candles to light the theatre, affecting the flow of air within the space, and the inability to deploy certain materials (such as smoking tobacco pipes), the workshop was highly revealing. For some audience members incense conjured up the scent of Catholic churches. For others the smell embodied a general non-denominational sense of religiosity. However, for at least some audience members (including myself) the mixture of burning frankincense and myrrh actually evoked the space of shops associated with new-age mysticism that sell incense alongside crystals, tarot cards, dreamcatchers and other spiritual paraphernalia. But the workshop also made clear just how

---

[11] This has resonances with some nineteenth-century scholars, such as Alois Riegl; see Beata Labuhn, 'Breathing a Moldy Air: Olfactory Experience, Aesthetics, and Ethics in the Writing of Ruskin and Riegl', *Future Anterior: Journal of Historic Preservation, Theory, and Criticism*, 13:2 (2016), pp. 103–17.

[12] Hans Ulrich Gumbrecht, *The Production of Presence: What Meaning Cannot Convey* (Stanford: Stanford University Press, 2004), p. 8.

[13] For an exploration of the Sam Wanamaker theatre, see Will Tosh, *Playing Indoors: Staging Early Modern Drama in the Sam Wanamaker Playhouse* (London: Bloomsbury, 2018).

[14] For more about the project, see 'Atmospheric Theatre', https://atmospherictheatre.exeter.ac.uk/ [accessed 05/08/2022].

much the relative heat of the incense, the degree of swing and movement of the censor, and the positioning of audience-members within the theatre all impacted on the precise moment at which the incense could be detected, the degree that it lingered, and therefore people's interpretation of the words, gestures and speech occurring on stage.

This kind of experimental approach suggested new insights about the smell of the past (the physical dispersal of scents in the theatre), smell and the past (the relative distance between contemporary and historical interpretations of the smell), and smell in the past (what the interaction between scent, uttered words and space might have meant to seventeenth-century noses). Experiencing the presence of incense in the theatre during the performance of a seventeenth-century play led my nose to new questions about the meanings of the scent – for example about the fate of this particular scent in a society with declining religious observance and a proliferation of heavily commercialized discourses around well-being, mindfulness and spirituality. Using our noses and engaging with smells can help us connect smell 'in', 'and' and 'of' the past in ways that generate new and exciting insights.

Such an approach takes us beyond History with a capital H as an academic discipline and requires a more interdisciplinary set of tools. Indeed, this is not just a book about or for historians, but for all interdisciplinary scholars interested in the past. It takes an approach that might be described as 'smell studies' or 'sensory studies' rather than smell or sensory history. Partly a survey of the existing scholarship on smell and the past and partly a set of ideas for the future of the field, it has been developed from conversations with and observations of the work of colleagues on the 'Odeuropa' project, an interdisciplinary endeavour involving scholars from computer science, heritage science and policy, art history and history, archaeology and anthropology, creative practice and more. The project, running from January 2021 to December 2023, aims to use data extracted from digitized texts and images to identify stories about European olfactory history and heritage from the 1600s to the 1920s and to bring those stories to the noses of scholars, museum and heritage professionals and public audiences.[15] The eye-opening and horizon-expanding opportunity to work alongside scholars in vastly

---

[15] For more on the Odeuropa project, see the website at: https://odeuropa.eu/.

different fields has provided the inspiration for the open methodological approach advocated in this book.

My aim is to convince the reader that when we study the past we should consider literally – and not just figuratively – following our noses in addition to deploying the 'common [ocular] *lens*' described in James's novel. To be clear, the argument here is not that we should try and directly re-experience the olfactory past. Rather, by engaging our noses, by sniffing the affordances of past olfactory presences, and by attempting to engage with historical ways of distinguishing and articulating smells, we may find new things out about the past or find alternative routes towards greater understanding. In this sense, the ideas discussed here find common cause with a wide range of scholarship that experiments with materiality in the present in order to think better about the past: including reconstructions that range from dance and costumes to artisanal recipes and scientific experiments.[16]

I am not arguing that we should abandon texts or an interpretative heuristic. I am making the case that we should smell as well as read, sniff out presence as well as meaning, and take a more open approach to the sensory methods we deploy in understanding the past. To dismiss the sense of smell as a tool for academics interested in the past is to take the easy road, a road that is readily navigable thanks to several centuries of depreciation, but – as we will see – making the case for the nose is more difficult. This should not stop us trying.

Given that my aim is to engage the noses of humanistic scholars, it is worth discussing the olfactory conditions under which this short publication has been produced.

It is significant that, as I write, we are (still) in the middle of an ongoing global pandemic. Smell-loss has been a widely reported symptom of Covid-19. The pandemic has ravaged the senses of many, leaving them with a reduced or distorted experience of smell and taste. Anosmia produces a loss of smell that also leads to an impaired ability to detect flavours. Parosmia produces distortions in the sense of smell that might lead once pleasant smelling things

---

[16] Andre Lepecki, 'The Body as Archive: Will to Re-enact and the Afterlives of Dance', *Dance Research Journal*, 42:2 (2010), pp. 28–48; Hilary Davidson, 'The Embodied Turn: Making and Remaking Dress as an Academic Practice', *Fashion Theory*, 23:3 (2019), pp. 363–99; Tianna Helena Uchacz, 'Reconstructing Early Modern Artisanal Epistemologies and an "Undisciplined" Mode of Inquiry', *Isis*, 111:3 (2020), pp. 606–13; Hjalmar Fors et al., 'From the Library to the Laboratory and Back Again: Experiment as a Tool for Historians of Science', *Ambix*, 63:2 (2016), pp. 85–97.

to smell bad. Phantosmia leads to olfactory hallucinations in which people perceive smells where there are none. The coronavirus outbreak has produced a huge global increase in individuals suffering from all three conditions. These conditions can leave lives empty: producing a loss of appetite, sleep and pleasure in daily pursuits that can lead to depression and, in extreme cases, suicidal thoughts.[17] The experience of the 'sensory desert' of anosmia, where everyday things lose their expected scent, has been described as a vertiginous experience of 'free fall' as the olfactory anchors of the world simply disappear.[18] There are many people who have lived – and will continue to live – with anosmia that they developed before the pandemic, through conditions unrelated to Covid-19. However, the spread of coronavirus has certainly highlighted the incredible disorientation and dislocation that the loss of our olfactory sense can bring about.

The response to the virus – social, economic, political – has also reshaped our olfactory worlds in meaningful ways. Mask-wearing has made us more attentive to the odours of our own breath and coloured our experience of ambient smellscapes.[19] The whiff of hand sanitizer has joined scents such as Turkish *kolonya* in signalling hygiene, encouraging feelings of safety or providing an olfactory reminder of the need for constant vigilance against infection.[20] Lockdowns have extracted us from our daily olfactory rhythms of work and leisure, causing a re-ordering of domestic smellscapes, and social distancing has made us more suspicious of scents that suggest an unwanted or dangerous intimacy with other people's bodies.[21] An increased emphasis on digital working practices and virtual sociability has resulted in a renewed attention to the scents that get left behind when life moves online. Home-scent kits have been devised to accompany virtual experiences, companies have marketed candles that recreate the smells of gyms or bars, and projects

---

[17] Rachel Herz, *The Scent of Desire* (London: HarperCollins, 2007), pp. 1–5.
[18] Paola Totaro and Robert Wainwright, *On the Scent* (London: Elliott & Thompson, 2022).
[19] Alison Young, 'The Limits of the City: Atmospheres of Lockdown', *British Journal of Criminology* (2021), doi: 10.1093/bjc/azab001; Sandro Felipe Santos Faria, 'Self-Perceived and Self-Reported Breath Odour and the Wearing of Face Masks during the COVID-19 Pandemic', *Oral Diseases* (2021), doi: 10.1111/odi.13958.
[20] Claudia Liebelt, 'Celebrating the Feast of Sweet Smells and Tastes during Corona Times', *Cultures of Hygiene*, https://culthygiene.hypotheses.org/126 [accessed 13/01/2022].
[21] Louisa Allen, 'The Smell of Lockdown: Smellwalks as Sensuous Methodology', *Qualitative Research*, doi: 10.1177/14687941211007663; Cynthia Sear, 'Porous Bodies', *Anthropology in Action*, 27:2 (2020), pp. 73–7.

have attempted to catalogue some of the scents of the 'old' normal and pandemic present as a 'new' normal begins to emerge.[22]

The pandemic has placed many scholars out of sniffing range of the remnants of the past: archives, museums, libraries and heritage sites. Often the scent of books we publish and read have been replaced by electronic equivalents, possibly accompanied by the whirr and dusty, burnt, scent of computer fans at our dining tables, on our beds, or, in more lucky cases in our deeply unequal profession, in our home offices. Many of us have witnessed a deodorization, re-odorization or re-ordering of our smellscapes. The endlessly proliferating range of online meetings, virtual get-togethers and web-based experiences seem comparatively scentless when measured against our previous ways of working and living.

However, in academic circles digital archives, tools and methods are not new. Over the last few decades, the digitization of the past – records and recordings, objects and images – has threatened to dematerialize (and deodorize) it. Just as the virtual lives of the pandemic helped produce a hankering for scents that helped tether people to 'reality', the digitization of the archive had already encouraged scholars to re-consider the role of scent. Both archivists and digital humanists have worried about the material qualities that are lost when we only engage with digitized, odourless, materials. They have speculated about the potential to transform digital data into smells and back again through processes of transduction and the possibility that smells might be preserved through analytical chemistry.[23]

If the increasingly digital nature of scholarly practice has caused a greater archival alertness to lost materialities that include smell, it has so far failed to produce an awareness of the relatively anosmic nature of disciplines that study the past. The study of the past has long excluded the evidence of the nose. Even now, despite an explosion of interest in smell and the past in recent years, this exciting and engaging work is still (with a few notable exceptions)

---

[22] For more on this, see Hannah McCann and William Tullett, 'The Pandemic Sensory Archive: Smell', www.archiveofintimacy.com/smell [accessed 13/01/2022]; William Tullett and Hannah McCann, 'Sensing the Pandemic: Revealing and Re-Ordering the Senses', *The Senses and Society*, 17:2 (2022), pp. 170–84.

[23] Charles Jeurgens, 'The Scent of the Digital Archive: Dilemmas with Archive Digitisation', *Bijdragen en mededelingen betreffende de beschiendenis der Nederlanden*, 128:4 (2013), pp. 30–54; William J. Turkel, 'Intervention: Hacking History, from Analogue to Digital and Back Again', *Rethinking History*, 15:2 (2011), pp. 287–96.

materially dry, textual and relatively scent-less. Within sensory humanities scholarship – where one might expect to find it – there is scant encouragement to use our noses and even less support for scholars who might wish to present their work through the medium of scent. We have passed the first stage of a sensory humanities, which is to 'add the senses [as another theme] and stir' and reached the second stage which understands the senses as socially and culturally contingent. However, we have yet to truly embrace a third wave that would involve not just the study *of* past senses but studying the past *with* the senses.[24] Despite developing, in part, from fears of digital dematerialization and a dissatisfaction with the discursive bent of the linguistic turn, sensory history remains curiously disembodied in its research methods and forms of dissemination.[25] The mind's nose has predominated over the body's.

From at least one perspective this seems quite remarkable. An impressive and intellectually vibrant community of scholars have been busy arguing that smell is important to how we understand the past.[26] The same community has exposed the epistemological and ontological shifts that have effaced or rejected the role of smell in the production, circulation and communication of particular forms of knowledge from the eighteenth century onwards.[27] There are plenty of critiques of the ocular-centric nature of our accounts of the past and calls to give attention to smell.[28] Yet whilst we have sought to rehabilitate representations of smell as an object of study, we have stopped short of using actual smells or deploying the nose as a tool. We talk the olfactory talk without walking the foul and fragrant walk.

Now seems a good moment to revise our scholarly practices in ways that are more sensorially diverse. When it comes to smell, we often do not know what we have until it disappears, or at least until it alters. Smells are creatures

---

[24] Ruth Tringham and Annie Davis, 'Doing Sensory Archaeology: The Challenges', in Robin Skeates and Jo Day (eds.), *The Routledge Handbook of Sensory Archaeology* (London: Routledge, 2020), p. 51.
[25] For sensory history as a reaction to the linguistic turn, see the discussion in C. Birdsall, J. F. Missfelder, D. Morat and C. Schleif, 'Forum: The Senses', *German History*, 32:2 (2014), pp. 256–8.
[26] The 'PastScent' directory and its associated bibliography illustrate the richness of this scholarship. See here for the directory https://odeuropa.eu/pastscent-membership/ and here for the bibliography, https://www.zotero.org/groups/4530561/pastscent/library [accessed 13/01/2022].
[27] For an overview of these arguments see Mark Jenner, 'Follow Your Nose? Smell, Smelling, and Their Histories', *American Historical Review*, 116:2 (2011), pp. 343–6.
[28] David Howes, Constance Classen and Anthony Synnott, *Aroma: The Cultural History of Smell* (London: Routledge, 1994), pp. 3–5; Jonathan Reinarz, *Past Scents: Historical Perspectives on Smell* (Chicago: University of Illinois Press, 2014), p. 4.

of change, and their emission signals a transition from one material, spiritual, symbolic or social state to another.[29] This observation is equally applicable not just to the emission but to the sensing of scents. People are most likely to be aware of their daily smellscapes at moments of transformation as new smells appear, old odours disappear, olfactory sensitivities alter, practices of sniffing change, or the temporal and spatial plotting of smells shift.[30]

As I have already suggested, the pandemic is one change that is producing a re-scenting and re-sensing of our worlds. But this is by no means the only such shift. For example, widening inequality and the march toward climate catastrophe have olfactory imprints and signature scents. If our understanding of the past is to mean something in the present and if it is to engage with the major issues of our time, then taking the humble (or rather historically *humbled*) nose seriously is essential.

Following this introduction, the main body of this text proceeds through three key sections. The first section, 'Noses', sets up the basic argument for why humanities scholars should use their noses. I describe using our noses as a process of 'articulating' the past. I argue that by developing our noses we may be able to better understand our own subject position as scholars, to re-odorize the archive's implicit odours and olfactory silences, and offer powerful ways of engaging those beyond the academy with our work.

The second section, 'Archives', explores the smells of archives, archives of smell and how we can utilize noses (human and otherwise) within them. Archives of smell exist, as do the methods to engage with them. However, I argue that discipline-specific distributions of the sensible, the anthropocentric bent of humanities research and an emphasis on a meaning-centred heuristic that values sources for their ability to be 'read' have all led scholars to ignore or devalue the potential of such archives. This section argues for a richer, more nose-wise, understanding of the types of archives we could build and the ways in which we can use existing archival resources.

---

[29] David Howes, 'Olfaction and Transition: An Essay on the Ritual Uses of Smell', *Canadian Review of Sociology*, 24:3 (1987), pp. 398–416; Martyna Śliwa and Kathleen Riach, 'Making Scents of Transition: Smellscapes and the Everyday in "Old" and "New" Urban Poland', *Urban Studies*, 49:1 (2011), pp. 23–41.

[30] For a brief discussion of this phenomena, see William Tullett, *Smell in Eighteenth-century England: A Social Sense* (Oxford: Oxford University Press, 2019), pp. 16–20.

The third section, 'Narrative', turns to the stories we currently and might tell about, through and with smell. Exploring some of the sensory-historical emplotments most often used in talking about smell's pasts, this chapter offers some suggestions about other – more radical – ways of revising the stories we tell about smell in or over time. It argues that to tell the story of the history of smell in a linear, historicist, way is to miss out on the essential multi-temporality of smell. By combining ideas about temporality from perfumery and history, it advances the claim that smell itself offers a potent way of structuring and communicating historical narratives.

At various points in the next pages you will be asked – if you are so inclined – to smell things. I call these moments 'Olfactory Figures'. Part of the argument of this book is that in doing you will add something to the ideas offered in the text. You might like to start by familiarizing yourself with own olfactory environments.

Olfactory Figure 0.1 *Breathe in your surroundings. Give your immediate environment a good sniff – both the ambient atmosphere and the objects around you. Does the space where you are reading this have a particular smell? How has this impacted your reading of this text so far?*

Getting you to consider the atmosphere in which we read and work is a central component of the next chapter. Smells, especially those around us on a daily basis in our work and home life, are often taken for granted. This is in part because we get used to odours fairly quickly. Think about the classic example of coming back from a holiday or a period away and realizing, as you cross the threshold, that your home has a distinctive smell. You had become used to it before but now, after spending time away, you have become desensitized to the smellscape. This Olfactory Figure is an opportunity for you to become attuned to your olfactory environment, to sniff actively rather than existing passively in your particular atmosphere and to consider the role it might play in your reading and thinking.

Take your time. When you are finished sniffing, we will continue onwards.

1

Noses

Articulating smell

Those that study smell and the past find themselves in a difficult methodological position. On the one hand, there is a general unwillingness to take our own noses or contemporary engagements with smells as an in-road into thinking about the past. Such direct engagements with scent tend to be shunted off into impact and public engagement activities (and even there they are criticized). On the other hand, if we rely on texts we are, as the pioneering sensory historian Alain Corbin recognized, the 'prisoners of language'.[1] In many cases (though certainly not all), this language is an impoverished one: in English it is difficult to describe smells and so we and our historical interlocutors often resort to emotive binaries (Disgusting! Delightful!) or material analogies (this smells like shit!).

I would like to argue that one plausible route out of this is that by attending more closely to our own noses and by using smells in our own work, we can begin to develop the types of knowledge and vocabularies that spring us from the linguistic lockup. By working with smells, we become better able to describe them, and being better able to describe smells will allow us to work with them more. Finally, building our smell knowledge and our ability to interpret smell-data makes us sensitive to new connections or implicit odours in the texts, images and objects that often form our main entry-points into understanding the past.

This starts with reflecting on our own olfactory subjectivities. We are used to suggesting that knowing the scholar is important for knowing their work.

---

[1] Alain Corbin, *Time, Desire, Horror: Towards a History of the Senses* (Cambridge: Polity, 1995), p. 190.

For humanities scholars, this has tended to mean their social background, politics and their broader body of academic research.[2] Archaeologists – who are used to getting their hands dirty – have a rich tradition of debate on the relative importance of the researcher's own embodied experience.[3] Recently, historians have also begun to attend to the fact that 'the historian is not presuming to feel what someone else may have felt; she is feeling for herself, through herself, in response to the past'.[4] Historians of emotions are paying more attention to the emotions they experience in the archive and their own feelings about the past's inhabitants.[5] The increasing desire to understand our subject-position as readers, writers and scholars has also been inspired by post-colonial studies, which have often invoked the words of Antonio Gramsci:

> The starting point of critical elaboration is the consciousness of what one really is, and is 'knowing thyself' as a product of the historical process to date, which has deposited in you an infinity of traces, without leaving an inventory ... therefore it is imperative at the outset to compile an inventory.[6]

Suggesting that we have different noses from historical actors and simply accepting the idea that we live in a more deodorized world in which we value smell less is not much of an inventory. It is, as contemporary studies of smell in the social sciences illustrate, to vastly underestimate the role of smell in everyday life.[7] Reading and writing about the past – the practices at the heart of an interpretative humanities – are experiences to which we bring our whole bodies, including our noses. We therefore need to understand the ways of smelling deposited in us by society, culture, history and our daily experience of life, work and leisure. The cultural and social conditioning of *our* sense of smell is a historical process that deserves unravelling.

---

[2] Edward Carr, *What Is History?* (Basingstoke: Palgrave Macmillan, 2001), p. 38.
[3] See the essays in Keates and Day (eds.), *The Routledge Handbook of Sensory Archaeology* (Abingdon: Routledge, 2020).
[4] Susan A. Crane, 'Historical Subjectivity: A Review Essay', *The Journal of Modern History*, 78:2 (2006), p. 452.
[5] Katie Barclay, 'Falling in Love with the Dead', *Rethinking History*, 22:4 (2018), pp. 459–73.
[6] Antonino Gramsci quoted in Edward Said, *Orientalism* (London: Penguin, 1995), p. 25.
[7] For example, see Christy Spackman and Gary A. Burlingame, 'Sensory Politics: The Tug-of-War between Potability and Palatability in Municipal Water Production', *Social Studies of Science*, 48:3 (2018), pp. 350–71.

This means compiling an inventory and that means describing what we smell, how we smell it and trying to understand how it informs our praxis. Other disciplines and non-academic experts offer models for this process. Smell-walks devised by art, architecture and design practitioners offer one way of thinking through our own olfactory subjectivities and environments.[8] Perfumery, wine tasting, coffee-grading and the odour-regulation industry all offer examples where training enables individuals to better discriminate and describe odours.[9] By smelling the scents contained in training kits and learning to articulate the differences between them perfumers quite literally – as well as metaphorically – become 'a nose'.[10] The more humanities scholars learn to smell, the more they learn to articulate smells in different ways, the better able they are to compile an inventory of the osmologies that have been deposited within them by past experience, and the more their own nose emerges into view.

Compiling this inventory involves tapping into the contemporary environmental and embodied sediments left by historical processes. Drawing on archaeological modes of thought, we can argue that all the smells that surround us today are the product of pasts that live on in the present. In other words, 'the past is the materiality of the present' and an understanding of olfactory pasts depends on understanding the 'way in which things, places and beings physically integrate what happens to them'.[11]

This is true in two senses. Firstly, the compounds that make up odorants existed in the past and they often continue to exist in the present. Two of the scents that we will discuss in the rest of this chapter – the rotten-egg scent of hydrogen sulphide and the acrid burned-match stink of sulphur dioxide – existed before human noses came into being and it is highly liked that they will still exist when homo-olfactus has disappeared. Near the very beginning of the

---

[8] C. Perkins and K. McLean, 'Smell Walking and Mapping', in S. M. Hall and H. Holmes (eds.), *Mundane Methods: Innovative Ways to Research the Everyday* (Manchester: Manchester University Press, 2020), pp. 156–73; Suzel Balez, 'Smell Walks', in E. Barbara A. Piga et al. (eds.), *Experiential Walks for Urban Design: Revealing, Representing, and Activating the Sensory Environment* (Cham: Springer, 2021), pp. 93–114.

[9] Asifa Majid et al., 'What Makes a Better Smeller?' *Perception*, 46:3–4 (2017), pp. 416–9; Anna Harris, *A Sensory Education* (London: Routledge, 2021), esp pp. 40–58.

[10] Bruno Latour, 'How to Talk about the Body? The Normative Dimension of Science Studies', *Body & Society*, 10:2–3 (2004), 205–29.

[11] Laurent Olivier, 'The Business of Archaeology Is the Present', in Alfredo Gonzalez-Ruibal (ed.), *Reclaiming Archaeology: Beyond the Tropes of Modernity* (London: Routledge, 2013), pp. 124, 128.

earth's existence these odours emerged from erupting volcanoes and oceans of blooming bacteria.[12] If climate change continues apace, then an excess of carbon dioxide may lead to the acidification of the oceans, the decomposition of marine life and the release of large amounts of hydrogen sulphide, which will poison the air and cause human extinction.[13] Our sense of smell will likely disappear before we do, since hydrogen sulphide exposure leads to anosmia (the loss of the sense of smell). These pungent scents were present at the birth of the earth. They will likely be a silent atmospheric presence at its death.

Secondly, olfactory perception in the present is the product of habits that have a history. The short space of time in which humans have existed on earth, between their first steps and their impending mass extinction, has been filled with a process in which communities and cultures have learnt to associate hydrogen sulphide and sulphur dioxide with particular meanings ranging from fears of hell to the smoggy moral quagmire of city life, have produced these odours through practices such as cooking and industrial production, and have learnt to respond to these scents in particular ways ranging from disgusted nose-holding to attempts to reduce the smoke that billows from factory chimneys. These assemblages of habits and meanings frame the possibilities for sensing in the present.

By taking this archaeological understanding of odour and by developing our nasal aptitude we become better readers of historical sources. Novels and other historical artefacts have historically acted like a perfume kit: they are sensitizing mechanisms that 'create more connections to the world by registering more differences in it'.[14] I want to suggest that by reversing the process we add even further to the ability to register differences. By developing our own noses, we may be able to register more differences in our historical sources and to recognize the odours that are sometimes implicit, obscured or unrecorded in texts. If we couple this with smelling recreations, reconstructions or close analogies of odours mentioned in historical texts or training ourselves

---

[12] Thomas Halliday, *Otherlands: A World in the Making* (London: Penguin, 2022), pp. 131, 138, 183, 242, 287.

[13] Jeff Tollefson, 'First Sun-dimming Experiment Will Test a Way to Cool Earth,' *Nature* 563 (2018), pp. 613–15; Weiqi Yao, Adina Paytan and Ulrich G. Wortmann, 'Large-scale Ocean Deoxygenation during the Paleocene-Eocene Thermal Maximum', *Science* 361:6404 (2018), pp. 804–6.

[14] Erica Fretwell, *Sensory Experiments: Psychophysics, Race, and the Aesthetics of Feeling* (Durham: Duke University Press, 2020), pp. 28–9.

to recognize qualities in smells according to past epistemologies, then we also develop an ability to register the differences between our own noses and those in the past. Far from trying to experience the worlds of historical actors, using the nose is a route into plotting precisely what might separate or align us with past noses. At the same time, we will become better able to understand that smells are one aspect of the materialities around us that act as the tip of an iceberg or the fossilized imprint of longer historical shifts in society and culture.

The stench of books and trees

The twinned olfactory history of books and pollution provides an instructive example when it comes to implicit odours outside of the text. Scholars often talk about the history of smell in terms of cleaning and deodorizing. We reflect rather less on the deodorizing tendencies within our own scholarship. The conversion of odours into words on a page is a kind of deodorizing process. In a discussion of the faecally rich work of the Marquis de Sade, Roland Barthes famously noted:

> Language has this property of denying, ignoring, disassociating reality: when written, shit does not have an odor; Sade can inundate his partners in it, we receive not the slightest whiff, only the abstract sign of something unpleasant.[15]

The relationship between words and smells is certainly more complicated than Barthes suggests: eighteenth-century authors noted the power of language to alter our impression of odours, contemporary psychologists have shown that the naming of odour can alter our experience of it, and reading odour words can activate the parts of our brains associated with both language and olfaction.[16] Nonetheless, we can still argue that reading a reference to the smell of hydrogen sulphide or sulphur dioxide, two common ingredients

---

[15] Roland Barthes, *Sade, Fourier, Loyola*, trans. Richard Miller (Berkeley: University of California Press, 1989), p. 137.
[16] William Tullett, *Smell in Eighteenth-century England: A Social Sense* (Oxford: Oxford University Press, 2019), p. 15; Asifa Majid and Stephen C. Levinson, 'The Senses in Language and Culture', *Senses and Society*, 6:1 (2011), pp. 8–9; Julio Gonzalez et al. cited in Emily Friedman, *Reading Smell in Eighteenth-century England* (Lewisburg: Bucknell University Press, 2016), p. 6.

in contemporary and historical pollution, does not have the same power as breathing them in or smelling a reconstruction of the associated scent.

Written down, pollution might not smell (or it might smell in a different way). However, the process of producing the books in which we read about the sensorial impact of pollution has long been the cause of foul odours. From its first inception to the present, the work of putting words on the printed page has stunk. Printer's workshops were proverbially odorous venues. In the sixteenth century, we find neighbourhood complaints against printers who stored odorous inks and varnishes outside their premises, whilst urine was used to soak printer's ink balls, clean type-faces and even as an ingredient in ink itself.[17] The intensifying industrialized production of paper added to this bouquet in the nineteenth century. The pulping that took place in paper mills emitted a range of gaseous pollutants into the air and waste chemicals into water sources. Nineteenth-century newspapers are littered with records of complaints about the smells of paper mills and the paper industry's own magazines took a keen interest in judicial wranglings over the odours emitted by paper production.[18] Those that worked in or lived near printing workshops and paper mills were exposed to offensive and potentially unhealthy smells.

In the twentieth and twenty-first centuries, paper mills have continued to emit a range of foul-smelling pollutants, including the 'Total-Reduced Sulphur' (TRS) that is partly responsible for acid rain. Historically it has not just been the pollutants themselves, but their further environmental impact, which has produced foul odours. For example, in 1904 after a paper mill was established at Örebro in Sweden, the discharge of fibres and chemicals into local water sources polluted local atmospheres and bodies of water. The result was beaches full of dead fish that 'smell[ed] bad, like paraffin oil'. Chemistry experts initially dismissed the pollution and argued that the smells of the mill and nearby river

---

[17] Ulla Lorenzo and De La Cruz Redondo, 'Women and Conflict in the Iberian Book Trade, 1472–1700', in Alexander Samuel Wilkinson and Graeme Kemp (eds.), *Negotiating Conflict and Controversy in the Early Modern Book World* (Leiden: Brill, 2019), p. 138; Mitchell M. Harris, 'The Expense of Ink and Wastes of Shame: Poetic Generation, Black Ink, and Material Waste in Shakespeare's Sonnets', in Andrea Feeser et al. (eds.), *The Materiality of Color: The Production, Circulation, and Application of Dyes and Pigments, 1400–1800* (Farnham: Ashgate, 2012), p. 71.

[18] 'St Thomas' Union', *Trewman's Exeter Flying Post*, 16th September 1874; 'Wortley Board of Guardians', *Sheffield Independent*, Saturday 4th August 1883; 'An Offensive Smell', *Blackburn Standard*, 20th January 1990; 'A Paper Mill Nuisance', *The World's Paper Trade Review*, 29:4 (1898), p. 1.

were no worse than 'cabbage plots in autumn' or 'cabbage soup'.[19] Whilst the emissions smelt bad, experts claimed they were not deadly. Throughout the twentieth-century paper mills across the globe have emitted strong, acrid, sulphurous odours that invaded surrounding homes and communities.[20] The growing obsession with online shopping, with the attendant explosion of cardboard production, has only increased the number of complaints about odour emissions from paper production sites, which in the United States are often located in majority black neighbourhoods.[21]

Hsuan Hsu has recently coined the phrase 'differential deodorization' to refer to the process by which the unequal distribution of atmospheric inequality produces both differently odorous environments and different awareness of environmental degradation and its impact on bodies.[22] For example, an exhibition held in Glasgow in 1910 by the Smoke Abatement Society aimed to promote electricity and included a section that detailed how the new 'smokeless, dustless, and odourless' electricity 'presented to the mind the pleasing picture of a smokeless city' and 'an atmosphere free from impurity'. On the same page sat a picture of St Andrews Cross power station in Glasgow, which was a coal-powered station generating electricity.[23] Electricity may have presented this imagined olfactory future to the mind, but it failed to present it to many noses: it merely took stench and pollution from middle-class kitchens and businesses, offering them a cleaner and odourless form of energy, whilst displacing that stench into the working-class neighbourhoods where power plants themselves were often built.[24] The history of energy transitions is one of differential deodorization.

---

[19] Kristina Soderholm, 'Environmental Awakening in the Swedish Pulp and Paper Industry: Pollution Resistance and Firm Responses in the Early 20th Century', *Business Strategy and the Environment*, 18 (2009), p. 37, 38.

[20] William Boyd, *The Slain Wood Papermaking and Its Environmental Consequences in the American South* (Baltimore: Johns Hopkins University Press, 2015), pp. 149–50, 172.

[21] Alana Semuels, 'Our Shopping Obsession Is Causing a Literal Stink', *Time*, 15th December 2021, https://time.com/6127646/box-factories-pollution/ [accessed 21/01/2022]; Emma Ockerman, 'Rotten Eggs, Paint, and Garbage: What Environmental Racism Smells Like', *Vice*, 9th December 2021, https://www.vice.com/en/article/7kb8ed/environmental-racism-cause-of-bad-smelling-neighborhoods [accessed 21/01/2022].

[22] Hsuan Hsu, *The Smell of Risk: Environmental Disparities and Olfactory Aesthetics* (New York: New York University Press, 2020).

[23] *Electricity: Lighting, Heating, Cooking and Power: Smoke Abatement Exhibition, 1910* (Glasgow: Corporation of Glasgow Electricity Department, 1910), p. 31.

[24] Peter Thorsheim, 'The Paradox of Smokeless Fuels: Gas, Coke, and the Environment in Britain, 1813–1949', *Environment and History*, 8:4 (2002), pp. 381–401.

The act of describing smells on the printed page can also be described as an act of differential deodorization, where the potentially-stench-producing manufacture of paper and the sanitizing properties of the written word enable the less olfactorily offensive experience of scholarly reading that takes place in libraries, offices and homes. The irony that you may be reading this text in paperback form is not lost on me as the author of this volume (and should give you, as the reader, pause for sniffing and thinking). We often romanticize the smell of old books and paper, the odour of which is released as their chemical components break down. This is a key smell associated with heritage. Yet this is only one stage in a book's longer olfactory-lifespan, an object biography that reveals very different and less fragrant olfactory stories.

In using our noses, we can situate our own place within wider processes and structures of olfactory inequality. Social and cultural historians are used to 'reading against the grain', looking inconsistencies, absences or contradictions in texts that might allow them to find the voices of women in documents produced by men or the agency of the subaltern in the archives of imperial bureaucracies. We can also learn to sniff against the grain, seeking out odours that are only implicit in our sources and their material forms, but which might become more obvious to a trained nose.

This practice of sniffing against the grain can also be applied to the contemporary politics of olfaction and used to understand its roots in particular pasts. To continue with our focus on pollution, we can turn to the example of car air-fresheners. The history of automobile design is partly one of ever more elaborate attempts at sensory cocooning and management. The acoustic enclosing of the car's interior from the sounds of roads, environments and the car itself was accompanied by attempts to curate the auditory atmosphere of the automobile using radios, CD players and sound systems.[25] A similar process was at work when it came to smell. Earlier automobiles often had open tops that meant one was exposed to the smells of the car and the environments one drove through. Recalling a family trip in a Morris Cowley in the 1920s, one Ronald Gene remembered being 'exposed to a variety of horrid industrial smells' as they drove through Birmingham.[26] However, an article in the

---

[25] Karin Bjisterveld et al., *Sound and Safe: A History of Listening behind the Wheel* (Oxford: Oxford University Press, 2014).

[26] Sean O'Connell, *The Car and British Society: Class, Gender and Motoring, 1896–1939* (Manchester: Manchester University Press, 1998), p. 81.

English magazine *Country Life*, published in 1901, noted that the 'vile smell' of the motor-car would soon be abated by the popularization of hoods and glass windows. These, the author suggested, would provide the same sensory insulation and comfort as sitting in a 'first-class railway carriage'.[27]

To some extent the author in *Country Life* guessed correctly. The olfactory experience of driving a classic car is very different from a modern one. Cars have become more insulated from the smells of their fuel so that it is no longer a constant, offensive, presence when driving but an occasional sniff – for example when refuelling before a long and exciting journey. Rather than being at the mercy of mechanical smells or being assaulted by odours from environments we drive through, the car has become a space for olfactory curation. From the 1950s onwards the interiors of vehicles were re-scented. In 1952, the 'Little Trees' car air freshener was invented by the German-Jewish chemist Julius Sämann, after hearing complaints from a milkman whose vehicle smelled of spoiled milk. The tree-shaped paper, scented with essential oils from evergreen trees and hung on a piece of string, would eventually lead to a whole industry based around car fragrance. We can describe this interlinked process as the product of 'air conditioning'. In using the term 'air-conditioning' I am referring not just to air conditioners but to a whole series of practices discussed by the German critic Peter Sloterdijk, who has traced modernity's obsession with the regulation and control of the atmosphere at multiple scales from the gas-mask to the air-conditioned building and from the gas chamber to the offshoring of toxic industries.[28]

This is one part of the history that helps understand Nissan's attempt – in 2013 – to use scent to promote its electric-only Leaf line of cars. Nissan hired the perfumer George Dodd and asked him to develop an 'aromatic blueprint of what the world could smell like in a zero emissions (ZE) future'. The description of the scent Dodd developed is telling:

> With inspiration gained from long walks amongst the Scottish Highlands, Dodd has concocted Nissan's 'future scent' with essences taken from cut green grass, myrtle oil, natural orange and the ineffable 'light as air' molecule. The scent evokes clean, fresh and organic landscapes in the minds of its sniffers, designed to encourage nostalgic feelings.

---

[27] 'Motoring', *Country Life Illustrated,* 4th May 1901, p. 575.
[28] Peter Sloterdijk, *Terror from the Air* (Cambridge: MIT Press, 2009).

The press release added that 'the futuristic scent is to be doused onto a LEAF shaped car air freshener ... and reminds recipients of what they are contributing to when driving their LEAF'.[29] The air freshener was intended to present past, present and future, through its constant, circumambient, scent – a reminder of past actions and an anticipation of the future they might produce. The scent was intended to evoke the pre-industrial heritage landscape of the Scottish Highlands with its floral, citrus and green notes. But it also unwittingly refers to human intervention in that landscape – it is, after all, *cut* grass. Whilst this scent is ostensibly about the future it also claims to encourage 'nostalgia'. Here there are elements of William Morris' 1890 utopia, *News from Nowhere*, in which Morris envisaged a future which was really a return to a late medieval golden age. In Morris' future, social rebirth is joined to ecological rebirth and the latter is accompanied by a particular smell-escape. The inhabitants of Morris' utopia reflect that their nineteenth-century forebears had 'submitted to live amidst sights and sounds and smells which it is in the very nature of man to abhor and flee from'. However, in the utopia they are surrounded by 'green forest scents' and the stench of manufacturing has disappeared: walking along a stream near Reading, Morris' narrator reflects that 'everything smelt too deliciously in the early night for there to be any of the old careless sordidness of so-called manufacture'.[30] Nissan's olfactory future contains within it similar assumptions about a golden-age – a future return to a desirable past – that features a natural, clean, undisturbed smell-scape. This is a nostalgia for an unpolluted past that may yet exist again.

However, we can also sniff the Nissan scent against the grain. Despite claims that the scent represents a fresh, green, future, the air-freshener is also the material product of practices that foreclose attempts to return to a natural, unpolluted, atmosphere. The manufacturing of fragrance materials today is largely dominated by a small number of companies. These companies have frequently been accused of polluting the areas around their factories with offensive and dangerous odours. In 2021 residents in the Murray Hill area of Jacksonville, in Florida, complained that for several years they had

---

[29] Nissan, 'Nissan Creates "Scent of Future"', https://europe.nissannews.com/en-GB/releases/nissan-creates-scent-of-the-future [accessed 31/03/2022].

[30] William Morris, *News from Nowhere and Other Writings* (London: Penguin, 2004).

been exposed to 'noxious turpentine-like fumes' that emerged from a local fragrance and flavour factory and infiltrated their homes. This caused 'a number of negative health impacts, including skin burning sensations, coughing, shortness of breath, dizziness, headaches, nausea, asthma attacks and insomnia'.[31] The same companies producing scents that represent a fresh, clean and unpolluted ecological future are being accused of serious pollution incidents that foreclose access to 'clean, fresh, and organic landscapes', to use the terms in Nissan's press release, for those that have the misfortune to live near factories and chemical plants.

The contrast here is important: the regulated atmospheres of Nissan's cars are filled with green scents while those living around chemical plants that produce synthetic fragrance are subject to intolerable and dangerous odours. One looks forward to a brave (old as much as new) ecological future while the other traps people in a polluted present. Nissan's futuristic air freshener is both an excellent example of Hsu's differential deodorization and a case study in how past-aware forms of sniffing against the grain can alert us to the implicit historical narratives and forms of atmospheric displacement embedded in contemporary olfactory cultures.

Archival absences

One reason olfactory stories are often only implicit is that they are infrequently written down or are only recorded in words with great difficulty. In 2005, a witness-seminar was held at King's College London on the impact of the 1952 London Smog, a pollution incident that may have caused as many as 12,000 deaths. The 1952 smog was a more extreme version of the many fogs and smogs that had clouded nineteenth and early twentieth-century London. One of the participants in the witness-seminar was Donald Acheson. At the time of the 1952 smog Acheson had been a medical officer at one of London's teaching hospitals, situated on Goodge Street just behind Tottenham Court Road. Commenting on his experience of the smog, Acheson did 'not recall

---

[31] Brendan Rivers, 'Residents "Appalled" as IFF Suggests It's Not Responsible for Odor Plaguing Murray Hill', https://news.wjct.org/first-coast/2021-03-25/residents-appalled-as-iff-suggests-its-not-responsible-for-odor-plaguing-murray-hill [accessed 31/03/2022].

any smell, but I do remember an eerie silence as there was little or no traffic'.[32] Medical writers in the 1950s, who were trying to ascertain the components of smogs and who had fixed on the acrid-smelling sulphur dioxide (SO_2) as a plausible culprit, had ready explanations for Acheson's odourless experience: the gases in smogs might cause smell-loss, 'sensitivity to smells often depends on the customary exposure and town dwellers would not be expected on the average to be as sensitive as rural dwellers'.[33] Investigations into the 1930 Meuse Valley fog in Belgium, in which sixty-two people and large numbers of animals died as a result of an industrial pollution incident, came to the same conclusion. Medics and meteorologists noted that inhabitants could not detect a distinctive smell to the fog, but the investigators from out of town could smell an acrid, sulphuric, scent in the air. The conclusion was simple: 'the inhabitants were deadened to the smell of this area'.[34]

That Londoners may have become habituated to the odour of their city's fogs is suggested in two further ways. Firstly, we are much more likely to find descriptions of London's fog that stress smell in accounts by travellers and visitors who were less used to its scent: Max Schlesinger described London's fog in the 1850s as 'thick, full of bad smells, and choking'; the Portuguese writer Eça de Queirós described the 'malodorous vapor' of London's fogs in the 1870s; and the American character in a Canadian-authored 1891 novel described London's smog as 'an abstract smell' without a distinguishable or nameable set of odours.[35] Secondly, some of the experimental methods for combatting the smog involved an assumption that the smog itself was in the olfactory background. In the 1950s, it was suggested that one of the components of smog – sulphuric acid – might be neutralized by ammonia. At this point you might like to sniff the following.

Olfactory Figure 1.1 *Sniff the ammonia in stale urine (human, cat) or smelling salts.*

---

[32] Virginia Berridge and Suzanne Taylor (eds.), *The Big Smoke: Fifty Years after the 1952 London Smog* (London: Centre for History in Public Health, London School of Hygiene and Tropical Medicine, 2005), p. 21.

[33] D. A. Layne, 'A Review on Smog', *Journal of the Royal Society of Health*, 75:2 (1955), p. 186.

[34] Friedrich Wolter, 'Die Nebelkatastrophe Im Maastal Sudlich Von Luttich', *Klinische Wochenschrift*, 10:17 (1931), p. 786; Kaj Roholm, 'The Fog Disaster in the Meuse Valley, 1930: A Fluorine Intoxication', *The Journal of Industrial Hygiene and Toxicology*, 19:3 (1937), pp. 126–37.

[35] Christine L. Corton, *London Fog: The Biography* (London: Harvard University Press, 2015), pp. 22, 157, 167.

Ammonia – in the form of stale urine – was a smell associated with fulling and tanning throughout the ancient, medieval and early modern periods.[36] But it is also the main ingredient in the smelling salts used throughout the early modern and modern periods to rejuvenate and enliven the senses.[37] Frequently contained in smelling bottles, ammonia – could be applied to the nose to give a rush by triggering the trigeminal nerve – a tactic still used by boxers and American football players today.

However, in the 1950s there were suggestions that it might also neutralize the dangerous elements of London's smogs. The evidence from Smithfield livestock show during the great smog suggested that cleanly cattle perished while less sanitary sheep and pigs were protected by the ammonia in their excrement. This was a similar sensory logic to the assertions in the previous three centuries that those living near tanner's yards, tobacconists, druggists, butchers and a host of other trades had been protected from seventeenth-century outbreaks of plague by the odoriferous effluvia emitted by their establishments.[38] Given the evidence from Smithfield (and experiments on literal guinea pigs) hospitals therefore trialled the use of bottles of ammonia with an adjustable wick which could be raised until there was 'a faint smell of ammonia in the room'. The smell, which patients described as 'fresh', was a sign that the smog had been present before the release of the ammonia and that a chemical change was clearing the air.[39] In other words, the presence of the smog that had been rendered inodorous to Londoners' habituated noses was made detectable by the processes used to combat it: the smell of ammonia made people aware of the smog despite their habituation to the latter's odours.

---

[36] Mark Bradley, '"It All Comes out in the Wash": Looking Harder at the Roman Fullonica', *Journal of Roman Archaeology*, 15 (2002), pp. 20–44; Yuanfa Dong et al., 'Multisensory Virtual Experience of Tanning in Medieval Coventry', *Eurographics Workshop on Graphics and Cultural Heritage* (2017), doi: 10.2312:gch.20171297; Julie Sanders, 'Under the Skin: A Neighbourhood Ethnography of Leather and Early Modern Drama', in Rory Loughnane and Edel Semple (eds.), *Staged Normality in Shakespeare's England* (Basingstoke: Palgrave Macmillan,), pp. 109–26.

[37] Tullett, *Smell in Eighteenth-century England*, pp. 172–5; Richard Howard Stamelman, *Perfume Joy, Obsession, Scandal, Sin: A Cultural History of Fragrance from 1750 to the Present* (London: Random House, 2009), p. 79.

[38] *A Treatise on Fevers* (London: Seagood and Collins, 1788), p. 71; Thomas Beddoes, *Essay on the causes, early signs and prevention of pulmonary consumption for the use of parents and preceptors. By Thomas Beddoes, M.D.* (Bristol, 1799), p. 34.

[39] 'Anti-Smog Bottle', *The British Medical Journal*, 5th November 1955, p. 1135; E. M Jones, C. Overy and E. M. Tansey (eds.), *Air Pollution Research in Britain c.1955–c.2000, Wellcome Witnesses to Contemporary Medicine*, vol. 58 (London: Queen Mary University of London, 2016), pp. 6–7.

Habituation is one reason for the relative invisibility of smell in the textual archive. However, historical shifts in attention and expertise have also made it more difficult for past and contemporary actors to identify and articulate the odours they encounter.

Since the eighteenth century, the once-solid link between foul smells and danger to health in medicine, law and public health had been slowly but surely worn away. Eighteenth-century medics and chemists began to distinguish between deadly gases and potentially misleading smells; mid-nineteenth-century sanitarians warned that getting rid of smells was no guarantee of getting rid of disease; and by the dawn of the twentieth century the rise of bacteriology had proceeded to wear away the final, strained, threads that connected the nose to determinations of danger.[40]

The growing use of synthetic scents produced in laboratories over the course of the nineteenth and twentieth centuries further destabilized the relationship between objects and smells, making it more difficult to ascertain what was mere odour and which scents might suggest dangerous gases. Several more recent examples testify to the confusion unleashed by the synthetic untethering of scent: in 2002 an advertising campaign for amaretto, which would have wafted its scent throughout the London underground, was halted because the UK Home Office worried that travellers would confuse the almond smell of the liqueur with the bitter almond scent associated with cyanide.[41] The nineteenth and twentieth centuries also saw industrial pollutants unleashed that possessed smells that were, like London's fog, difficult to describe: both perfumery and pollution increasingly emitted 'abstract' scents.

Finally, our sensorial relationship to food and produce altered from the late eighteenth century onwards: invisible calories and chemical constituents replaced sensorial properties as guides to food's nutritional benefit, populations were detached from the processes and venues where food production took place, and smell became more important in creating enticing atmospheres

---

[40] Tullett, *Smell in Eighteenth-century England*, pp. 66–87; William Tullett, 'Re-Odorisation, Disease, and Emotion in Mid-nineteenth-century England', *The Historical Journal*, 62:3 (2019), pp. 765–88; Melanie Kiechle, *Smell Detectives: An Olfactory History of Nineteenth-century Urban America* (London: University of Washington Press, 2017), pp. 259–65.

[41] Louise Jury, 'Whiff of Almond Falls Victim to Terror Alert', *The Independent*, 14 November 2002, https://www.independent.co.uk/news/media/whiff-of-almond-falls-victim-to-terror-alert-133417.html [accessed 25/01/2022].

than in the assaying of quality and freshness.⁴² We have inherited bodies – and noses – which are an archive of these social and cultural shifts in attention and increasing olfactory abstraction.

Many populations have also been taught to ignore or even to value the smells of pollution as the smells of progress, industry and gainful employment. A Welsh writer to the *Wrexham Advertiser* in 1869 sought to defend the local paper mill where they worked, which had been threatened with closure for causing an olfactory nuisance – on the grounds of economy: they admitted that there was a distinctive smell emitted by the mill but argued that 'none of us poor people feels a bit the worse for it, but nigh two hundred of us is to be turned adrift for the sake of ten or twelve'.⁴³ It has been demonstrated that for many nineteenth-century ears the 'noise' of factories was the sweet sound of progress, industry and economic growth.⁴⁴ Across the nineteenth and twentieth centuries populations have also been instructed – with varying degrees of success – that the smells of pollution were in fact the sweet 'smell of prosperity'.⁴⁵ Growing up in Piedemont West Virginia in the 1950s, Henry Louis Gates Jr described how the

> acrid, sulfurous odor of the … paper mill drifts along the valley, penetrating walls and clothing, furnishings and skin. No perfume can mask it. It is as much a part of the valley as is the river, and the people who live there are not overly disturbed by it. 'Smells like money to me', we were taught to say in its defence, even as children.⁴⁶

The ability to detect, name and describe an odour and to connect it to pleasure and danger, the question of whose nose is taken seriously, is always bound up with what Jacques Rancière has termed a 'distribution of the sensible' that values the senses of some over others.⁴⁷ This 'distribution of the sensible' determines which descriptions of odour we find in archival sources. Opening

---

[42] Steven Shapin, '"You Are What You Eat": Historical Changes in Ideas about Food and Identity', *Historical Research*, 87:237 (2014), pp. 390–1; Adam Mack, '"Speaking of Tomatoes": Supermarkets, the Senses, and Sexual Fantasy in Modern America', *Journal of Social History*, 43:4 (2010), p. 828.

[43] 'Bersham Paper Mills', *Wrexham Weekly Advertiser*, 19th September 1868.

[44] Mark M. Smith, *Listening to Nineteenth-Century America* (Chapel Hill: University of North Carolina Press, 2001), pp. 136–7, 140–1.

[45] Noga Morag-Levine, *Chasing the Wind: Regulating Air Pollution in the Common Law State* (Oxford: Princeton University Press, 2003), pp. 129, 134.

[46] Henry Louis Gates Jr., *Colored People: A Memoir* (London: Penguin, 1995).

[47] Jacques Rancière, *The Politics of Aesthetics*, trans. Gabriel Rockhill (London: Bloomsbury, 2013).

our noses and learning about the kinds of smells that may have been present, but that went unrecorded for various reasons, is one way of countering that tendency.

Material presences and olfactory affordances

This is equally true for the more-than-human world. Relying on the textual remnants of human olfactory perception in historical sources that are mediated by shifting forms of attention, habituation and sensitivity can justly be criticized for its anthropocentrism. For example, urban spaces – contemporary and historical – contain innumerable 'canine cartographies' that dogs can sniff out, but which humans ignore despite their tendency to consciously and subconsciously communicate through scent in similar ways.[48] We should not just attend to our own noses but to the more-than-human ones that have sniffed (and continue to sniff) out different olfactory traces in the environment. Modern understandings of animal sensoria can, when deployed with careful contextualization crafted from an understanding of past cultural and material worlds, aid us in understanding past animal experiences.[49]

This requires an engagement with what we might call, to coin a phrase, 'the molecular commons'. Once we turn to the more-than-human world the idea that many human cultures struggle to communicate smells in language comes up against the fact that for huge swathes of life on earth smell *is* the common language: the volatile organic compounds that make up smell are a multispecies lingua-franca. We are embedded in a vast web of chemical communications between species in which smelling and odorants play a prime role.

Dogs provide an apt example of how humans have intervened, policed and politicized the molecular commons. On the one hand, humans have attempted to control molecular interactions between dogs because of their smell: the use of urine in canine communications gained the attention of human city dwellers in the nineteenth century, who attempted to clean and disinfect the

---

[48] Chris Pearson, 'A Walk in the Park with Timmy: History and the Possibilities of Companion Species Research', *The Wild*, 1 (2009), 87–96; Inbal Ravreby, Kobi Snitz and Noam Sobel, 'There Is Chemistry in Social Chemistry', *Science Advances*, 8:25 (2022), eabn0154.
[49] Erica Fudge, 'Milking Other Men's Beasts', *History and Theory*, 52 (2013), pp. 12–28.

information-rich effluent found on their streets and doorsteps (though not necessarily successfully).[50] On the other hand, dogs have been used as sensory prostheses that allow access to aspects of the molecular commons that have been thought to evade detection by the human nose: hunting prey, detecting disease and catching criminals. In the Atlantic world during the eighteenth and nineteenth centuries dogs were honed as a form of biopower that could sniff out runaway slaves. Slave communities responded by using red pepper, onions, earth, turpentine, water and the scent of other prey including rabbits to cover their tracks.[51] Perhaps ironically, given claims about modernity's dismissal of smelling as a route to knowledge, during the twentieth-century sniffer dogs were represented as a tool of modern scientific detection in a colonial context, where they could be used without the opposition they encountered in European metropoles.[52] Authorities were able to do this by transferring responsibility for truth-telling from human to canine noses and black-boxing the unchallenged (mythical) quality of canine olfactory accuracy. Today, despite the high number of false alerts and concerns about sensorial privacy, sniffer dogs continue to be used in ways that racially profile segments of the population and extend state surveillance of the molecular commons.[53] The atmosphere and the volatile organic compounds that inhabit it are an intensely political space and have provided – continue to provide – resources for policing and, as slave communities showed, resistance.

Odorous molecules are a communicative resource that have been and are being drawn on by lifeforms across the earth to different ends. Whilst dogs provide an example in which human agency is central, in other cases

---

[50] Chris Pearson, *Dogopolis: How Dogs and Humans Made Modern New York, London, and Paris* (Chicago: University of Chicago Press, 2021), pp. 164–5, 170–6.

[51] Tyler D. Parry and Charlton W. Yingling, 'Slave Hounds and Abolition in the Americas', *Past and Present*, 246:1 (2020), pp. 69–108.

[52] Keith Shear, 'Police Dogs and State Rationality in Early Twentieth-century South Africa', in Lance van Sittert and Sandra Swart (eds.), *Canis Africanis* (Leiden: Brill, 2008), pp. 193–216; Binyamin Blum, 'The Hounds of Empire: Forensic Dog Tracking in Britain and Its Colonies, 1888–1953', *Law and History Review*, 35:3 (2017), pp. 621–65; Neil Pemberton, '"Bloodhounds as Detectives" Dogs, Slum Stench and Late-Victorian Murder Investigation', *Cultural and Social History*, 10:1 (2015), pp. 69–91.

[53] Shontel Stewart, 'Man's Best Friend? How Dogs Have Been Used to Oppress African Americans', *Michigan Journal of Race and Law*, 25 (2020), pp. 199–201; Amber Marks, 'Drug Detection Dogs and the Growth of Olfactory Surveillance: Beyond the Rule of Law?', *Surveillance & Society*, 4:3 (2007), pp. 257–71; Mark Neocleous, 'The Smell of Power: A Contribution to the Critique of the Sniffer Dog', *Radical Philosophy*, 167 (2011), pp. 9–14.

non-human actors draw on the molecular commons to pursue their own particular goals. As a demonstration of this at work, you might like to smell.

Olfactory Figure 1.2 Sniff truffles or, more likely, truffle oil.

Fungi communicate with both each other and the world around them via odorous compounds. It has been suggested that 'through smell, we can participate in the molecular discourse fungi use to organize much of their existence'.[54] For example, truffles emit a scent that contains 5-alpha-androstenol, which is also contained in male perspiration, female urine and a secretion that male pigs use to signal their sexual availability.[55] The latter is why female pigs are often used as skilled truffle-hunters. By enticing animals to eat and, in due course, excrete them truffles ensures their reproduction through the spread of their spores. Humans, pigs and fungi are (and have been) enmeshed in a desirous multispecies web of chemical communication through smell: we have long existed in multi- and inter-species 'fields of odor' that 'overlap with one another like ghosts at a disco'.[56]

Understanding the molecular commons and its implications for studying the past requires a particular methodological disposition on the part of researchers. Taking the interspecies communications revealed by smell seriously – observing it in more-than-human actors and, where possible, digging our own noses into those conversations – constitutes one part of the 'art of noticing' advocated in Anna Lowenhaut Tsing's study of the matsutake mushroom. The presence of the matsutake mushroom's smell has spurred (and has been spurred by) a whole series of historical processes of mobility, consumption and terraforming that have crossed species barriers. The nostalgia-evoking properties of that smell for many people in Japan today are the product of these longer historical developments that stretch back beyond the initial memory-laden sniff in the twenty-first century all the way to the eighth century.[57] Noticing

---

[54] Merlin Sheldrake, *Entangled Life: How Fungi Make Our Worlds, Change Our Minds, and Shape Our Futures* (London: Vintage, 2020).
[55] Laura U. Marks, 'Thinking Multisensory Culture', in Francesca Bacci and David Melcher (eds.), *Art and the Senses* (Oxford: Oxford University Press, 2011), p. 241.
[56] Sheldrake, *Entangled Life*.
[57] Anna Lowenhaupt Tsing, *The Mushroom at the End of the World: On the Possibility of Life in Capitalist Ruins* (Oxford: Princeton University Press, 2015), pp. 45–52; Matsutake Worlds Research Group, 'Strong Collaboration as a Method for Multi-sited Ethnography: On Mycorrhizal Relations', in Mark-Anthony Falzon (ed.), *Multi-sited Ethnography: Theory, Praxis, and Locality in Contemporary Research* (Farnham: Ashgate, 2009), p. 211.

contemporary responses to the scent of the matsutake mushroom and the environments in which it grows reveals a much longer history that becomes apparent when we follow our noses into the past.

However, the last two centuries of life on earth have seen a tragedy of the molecular commons as pollution, projects of deodorization and forms of chemical manipulation including the use of pesticides have reshaped the constitution of – and restricted access to – the molecular commons. Bees are one example that illustrates the pincer movement against both perception and environment in practice. On the one hand, pesticides have been shown to alter the part of the brain that bees use for learning, meaning that they forget the smell of food.[58] On the other hand, polluted fumes from traffic have been shown to destroy the chemicals in some flowers. This means the flowers are rendered unrecognizable to bees who are hunting for food.[59] This is the tip of the iceberg, perhaps an apt metaphor in this context that illustrates how the wider reshaping of noses and odorants has been transforming eco-systems.

The decline of the molecular commons provides one compelling meta-narrative for thinking about the shifting relationship between humans, nature and smell over time. From petrol, pesticides and coal-fired power stations to soaps, disinfectants and petrochemical pollutants, the nineteenth and twentieth centuries saw vast changes to the chemistry of local and global atmospheres. Opening our noses – and taking the nose-witnesses around us seriously – opens up routes for histories of inter-species chemical relationality.

In order to fully appreciate all of these stories, we must take our noses out of our books and pay attention to the odorous histories that are often only implied by, or even explicitly denied, in texts. Later on in the same testimony we quoted earlier, Donald Acheson, the medical officer who lived through London's smogs, added: 'I don't recall a smell of SO_2 which according to history I should have been able to smell.'[60] Acheson's comments may unwittingly point to one more reason why engaging our sense of smell can help scholars interested in

---

[58] Sarah M. Wiliamson and Geraldine A. Wright, 'Exposure to Multiple Cholinergic Pesticides Impairs Olfactory Learning and Memory in Honeybees', *The Journal of Experimental Biology*, 216:10 (2013), 1799–807.

[59] Inka Lusebrink et al., 'The Effects of Diesel Exhaust Pollution on Floral Volatiles and the Consequences for Honey Bee Olfaction', *Journal of Chemical Ecology*, 41 (2015), pp. 904–12; James M. W. Ryalls, 'Anthropogenic Air Pollutants Reduce Insect-Mediated Pollination Services', *Environmental Pollution*, 297 (2022), p. 118847.

[60] Berridge and Taylor, *The Big Smoke*, p. 22.

the past. Odorants are always having an influence, even if that influence may not be vocalized, textualized, visualized or felt by those that live with them for extended periods of time. Humanities scholars can play a role in resurrecting those odours, bringing them back to the nose and considering their impacts. To appreciate the sensory labour, inequalities and environmental changes embedded in historical processes we have to reverse the effects of differential deodorization and habituation that have rendered them less obvious and more difficult to articulate in our disciplines. At this point, you might like to sniff the following.

Olfactory Figure 1.3 *Light a safety match, blow it out and sniff the smoke.*

One of the molecules you are sniffing here is the scent that Donald Acheson said he should have smelled in 1950s London: sulphur-dioxide. In this case SO_2 is the by-product of the chemical reaction caused when you light a match. The sulphurous smoke emitted by matches was one reason why earlier, nineteenth-century, friction matches were called 'lucifers' – a slang term that continued into the twentieth and twenty-first centuries – thus playing on the long-running link between sulphurous smells and hell. Sulphur dioxide is also belched out by volcanoes in prodigious quantities, which have no doubt furthered the connection between underworlds and pungent smoke. But sulphur dioxide is also a component of historical pollution, including London's nineteenth- and twentieth-century fogs, the 1930 Meuse Valley disaster, and the 1948 Donora smog that devastated the respiratory health of at least 6,000 people in Pennsylvania.

In 1969 a resident of the US city of St Louis wrote to a Senate subcommittee on pollution. She worried that she had become used to the sour smells of nearby factories and this had caused her to ask, 'What does air smell like?'[61] Developing and training our noses through acts of smelling will better enable historians to articulate what air and the various elements floating within it smell 'like' both today and in the past. The more we use our noses, the more we can link odours to ever-growing fields of meanings, then the more we will be able to link those odours to historical objects, images or texts in ways that

---

[61] Richard L. Revesz and Jack Lienke, *Struggling for Air: Power Plants and the 'War on Coal'* (Oxford: Oxford University Press, 2016), p. 25.

might, on first glance, be hidden from us. The more we attend to our noses and learn to sniff, the more we are be able to bring the historical sources we use into mutual *relation* with smells – both past and present.

It is often noted that the sensory historian must be attentive to the 'frontier between the perceived and the unperceived, and, even more, of the norms which decree what is spoken and what left unspoken'.[62] To fully understand what is unspoken – because sensitive actors could not or were not allowed to speak – we must take an imaginative and epistemological leap into thinking with the olfactory presences of the past, the material presences that are not meaning but which provided the context in which meaning-making may have happened. This also involves understanding the presence of the absence of smell – the odours that might be missing from spaces or unperceived. The absence of smell can often be just as influential as its presence: for example, in a hospital a relative lack of odour can be experienced as an olfactory lack, a sense of relief, an indicator of care or a source of composure.[63]

In attending to material presence and presence of absence through smell we can turn to our contemporary understanding of olfactory materialities and our own noses in order to help us understand the atmospheric affordances of the past. In disciplines like archaeology, where the material past is at the centre of research, this focus on sensory affordances has already been advocated.[64] If we can understand – indeed attempt to smell – some of the odorous compounds associated with the presence of particular plants or animals, the effluvia that have been emitted by particular industrial processes, or the scents that have emerged from particular perfumes, textiles, foods or sources of heat and lighting (to name but a few examples), then we can begin to build up an olfactory appreciation of these material affordances.

These affordances produce a complex dance of agencies. The study of material culture has increasingly attended to the agency of objects and the

---

[62] Alain Corbin, 'Charting the Cultural History of the Senses', in David Howes (ed.), *Empire of the Senses: The Sensual Culture Reader* (Oxford: Breg, 2005), p. 135.
[63] Anette Stenslund, 'A Whiff of Nothing: The Atmospheric Absence of Smell', *The Senses and Society*, 10:3 (2015), 341–60.
[64] Yannis Hamilakis, *Archaeology and the Senses: Human Experience, Memory and Affect* (Cambridge: Cambridge University Press, 2014); Heather Hunter-Crawley, 'Classical Archaeology and the Senses: A Paradigmatic Shift?', in Robin Keates and Jo Day (eds.), *The Routledge Handbook of Sensory Archaeology* (London: Routledge, 2020), pp. 441–2.

ways in which they provoke responses, guide action, or construct and maintain human relationships. In both past and present odour has been understood as troublesome and slippery form of materiality that requires human intervention to control, channel or destroy it.[65] Odours are a form of material power that lend agency to the material world and that can 'aid or destroy, enrich or disable, ennoble or degrade us' and that therefore call for 'attentiveness, or even "respect"'.[66] But we can go further than this. The scents around us are one way in which we become a fungible part of the material world: we are not simply acted on by the world but instead become intermingled with it. As Annemarie Mol argues for food, when I engage with my environment through sniffing and breathing, 'I do not first and foremost apprehend my surroundings, but become mixed up with them' in a 'transformative engagement of semipermeable bodies with a topologically intricate world'.[67]

As contemporary research on the atmospheric components of war, pollution and state-sponsored repression has shown, 'seen from the outside they are measurable objects, seen from within they are experiential conditions of optical blur and atmospheric obscurity'.[68] When we draw on textual descriptions of sniffing we are smelling from the outside in a doubled sense, as olfactory experiences are mediated first by past acts of writing them down and again by our reading of them in the present. Engaging our noses with smells gives us a new and different way of attending to the materiality of the past by asking us to consider what it means to exist within or as part of the flows of material world rather than as an outsider interacting with it.

All of this requires us to pay olfactory attention. As Anna Harris makes clear in her guide to educating our senses, Tsing's 'art of noticing' shares a great deal with similar concepts developed by a mix of scholars including Tim Ingold's 'education of attention', Bruno Latour's training 'to be affected' and Marilyn Strathern's 'learning to see'.[69] All of these emphasize that by learning to use our

---

[65] Victoria Henshaw, *Urban Smellscapes: Understanding and Designing City Smell Environments* (London: Routledge, 2013).

[66] Jane Bennett, *Vibrant Matter: A Political Ecology of Things* (Durham, NC: Duke University Press, 2010), p. ix.

[67] Annemarie Mol, *Eating in Theory* (Durham, NC: Duke University Press, 2021), p. 30.

[68] Forensic Architecture, 'Cloud Studies', https://forensic-architecture.org/investigation/cloudstudies [accessed 25/08/2020].

[69] Anna Harris, *A Sensory Education* (London: Routledge, 2020), pp. 4–6.

senses and developing sensate skills we acquire new ways of apprehending our sources – be they textual, auditory, visual or material. Over the course of the chapter so far, I have offered up several ways in which the art of noticing would enrich the interdisciplinary study of smell. Noticing means sensitizing ourselves to those odours that we – or individuals and communities in the past – do not attend to thanks to habitation, fatigue, and the distribution of the sensible. Noticing means taking seriously the perceptions of other non-human actors, how they respond to the odours around us and how we might engage with those same scents. Finally, noticing means that by learning to sniff our environments and building up our olfactory knowledge we may become attuned to the implicit scents that may be hiding, in front of our noses, in our textual and material evidence. All of these take us beyond the straw-person idea that using our noses involves an assumption that we can or should be able to 'smell the past'.

Re-odorizing the material archive

This also means bringing smells back into play with historical environments and material culture. In order to explore this, we can consider the linked examples of classic cars and industrial heritage. The smell that links both of these is the smells producing by fuel – petrol and coal. Both industrial heritage spaces and classic cars are in the process of losing or have already lost many of their important odours. This is for sound ecological reasons. But it should force us to consider how we could preserve or represent the smells of these fuels in the future. Producing what I call 'olfactory fascimiles', synthetic reproductions of the odours given off by fuels, is one route into doing this. Remaking odours that can be used without the need to burn coal at industrial heritage sites or pump petrol into cars would mean that we can understand these spaces and vehicles in their olfactory context.

    This is important because the smell of petrol is integral to the history of the motor car and the experience of driving. Whilst we tend to invoke Proust's madeleine when we talk about smell and memory, there is a far better and more interesting quote that illustrates the mnemonic power of odour in Proust's ouvre. In an essay in *Contre Sainte-Beuve*, written between 1895 and 1900, Proust remembers a particular odour spilling through his open window:

At times the rank smell of petrol came in – that smell which spoils the country, according to modern thinkers who believe that the human soul can exercise free will as to what brings joy to it, etc., who believe that truth is objective, not subjective. But the perceived is so instantly transformed by the perceiver that the smell of petrol came into my room quite simply as the most intoxicating of all the summer smells of the country, the smell that summed up both its beauty and the joy of speeding over it, of being on one's way to a longed-for destination. Even the smell of hawthorn would but have called up in my mind a sort of motionless, circumscribed happiness, a happiness tethered to a hedge. That delicious smell of petrol, sky-coloured, sun-coloured petrol, was the whole vast stretch of the countryside, and the joy of setting out.[70]

Proust's point here is that even a malodour – or a scent socially coded as a malodour – can evoke a deeply pleasant memory. Nostalgia, memory and heritage have the potential to transform scents from malodours that offend to fragrances that bring joy to heart of those that smell them.

Certainly, petrol and car fumes were initially coded as unpleasant scents. The introduction and popularization of motor cars in the early decades of the twentieth century brought many olfactory complaints linked to human and non-human noses. In 1903, Colonel Daniells, chief constable of Hertfordshire in England, noted that there was opposition in rural areas to automobiles and that 'much of the prejudice has been caused by the alarm of horses at the sight and smell of motor-cars'. However, he reasoned that horses would quickly become accustomed to their new fellow road-users.[71] Indeed, a 1901 letter to *The Times* by Sir Edmund Monson, then in Paris, noted a belief that French horses had quickly got used to the 'sight, sound, and smell' of automobiles. However, he also suggested that human travellers often complained of the 'asphyxiating odours' that caused cars to resemble, 'a diabolical phenomenon', the 'stench' of which disrupted the enjoyment of Parisians out for rural rides in horse-drawn carriages.[72]

---

[70] Marcel Proust, *On Art and Literature, 1896–1919*, trans. Sylvia Townsend Warner (New York: Dell, 1964), p. 48.
[71] Henry Norman, 'Motorists and the Public', *The World's Work*, 2 (1903), p. 124.
[72] Sir Henry Thompson, *The Motor-car: An Elementary Handbook on Its Nature Use & Management* (London: F. Warne and Company, 1902), pp. 20–1.

Many authors reasoned that the future of motoring would be far less odorous. In a 1913 book, one Mr Herbert Gubbins predicted what life would be like in London in 2905 AD. In this far future, air travel would become popular because, unlike automobiles, they would not 'pollute the air with vile odours'. Travel through the air would, Gubbins predicted, become a 'wonderful sensation' and there would be no more 'crawling along a road at eighty miles an hour in an evil-smelling motor-car'.[73] Others predicted that better upkeep of cars would mean that future motorists would have a less offensive olfactory impact. A 1901 review of a book on car maintenance in the London-based journal *The Athenaem* compared the possible advantages and disadvantages of steam-, electricity- and petrol-fuelled automobiles. Coming down firmly in favour of petrol vehicles, the author noted:

> The main objection to these, the smell they leave in their wake, is rapidly becoming a thing of the past. The older types give off bad odours; but where this is found to be the case with a motor car, it is almost invariably due to the insufficient attention paid to keeping the parts clean.[74]

Early-twentieth-century debates over the best way of fuelling automobiles often touched on the question of smell. At a London meeting of the Institution of Electrical Engineers in 1914 a member noted that the

> already extensive adoption of the petrol type of commercial vehicle … has brought in its train conditions which, I suppose, everybody will agree have not added to the amenities of city life. The noise and smell from that class of vehicle have frequently been the cause of bitter complaint.[75]

There was an expectation that, whilst contemporary cars smelt bad, future ones would not suffer from the same issues.

If we fast-forward to the present, then those predictions seem oddly prophetic. The growth of electrical vehicles may contribute to the slow removal of the smells of petrol from motoring life. However, this will not be without

---

[73] Herbert Gubbins, *The Elixir of Life: Or, 2905 A.D.; a Novel of the Far Future* (London: H.J. Drane, 1914), pp. 94–5.
[74] *The Athenaeum*, no. 3832, 6th April 1901, p. 346.
[75] F. Ayton et al., 'Discussion on Electric Battery Vehicles before the Institution, 19th March, 1914', *The Journal of the Institution of Electrical Engineers*, 52:232 (1914), pp. 495-6; A. Page et al., 'Discussion on "Electric battery vehicles" before the Scottish Local Section, 24th March, 1914', *The Journal of the Institution of Electrical Engineers*, 52:234 (1914), p. 649.

resistance. In July 2021, the car manufacturer Ford announced that it had commissioned a fragrance. Whilst not on sale publicly, the scent was designed to help sell electric cars to consumers who were still attached to the sensory trappings of petrol-powered vehicles. A survey had been commissioned by the company in which 'almost 70 per cent' of respondents had claimed 'they would miss the smell of petrol to some degree' and the scent – which combined smells of rubber, car interiors, and fuel with more common fragrance notes – was intended to 'give them a hint of that fuel-fragrance they still crave'.[76]

So, contrary to early-twentieth-century predictions, the smell of petrol has not gone away. In fact, it has gone from being seen as a nuisance to engineer out of cars to a smell that people value, desire and want to preserve. Recent attempts to encourage classic car owners, a large heritage community, to convert to more eco-friendly fuels or even to swap out their petrol-powered engines for electric ones have often met with refusal because the key attraction of classic cars is their sensory appeal – including their smells. For example, one classic car owner Andrew Fawkes noted in the right-wing magazine *The Spectator* that converting his 1968 Aston Martin to an electric engine would mean losing the 'old car smell':

> That heady mixture of leather, wood, old cigars, fuel, exhaust smoke and countless other sources that have woven themselves into the carpets, seats and headlining of your classic car. It can't be bottled but it's universally loved.[77]

The changing smell of fuel – especially petrol – is clearly integral to the olfactory histories in which automobiles are embedded. However, in the future we may not want to or be able to run classic cars on the fuels that would have originally contributed to their distinct scent and the sensory experience of motoring for reasons of either conservation or environmental care.

The same issue rears its head in the case of industrial heritage. If you visit Cambridge you could visit the Cambridge Museum of Technology. The museum is housed in an old sewage pumping station built in 1894, where the massive Hawthorn-Davey engines used to cleanse and deodorize the

---

[76] Ford Press Release, 'Splash and Dash; Ford Fragrance Shows petrol Fans they Won't miss Out with Mustang Mach-E GT', 15th July 2021, https://media.ford.com/content/fordmedia/feu/en/news/2021/07/14/ford-mach-eau.html [accessed 01/03/2022].

[77] Martin Gurdon, 'Should you electrify your classic card?', *The Spectator*, 3rd November 2021, https://www.spectator.co.uk/article/can-classic-cars-go-electric/ [accessed 01/03/2022].

waters of Cambridge can still be found. Ironically, the engines themselves, no longer running, sitting in silence, have also been somewhat deodorized. You can still smell the tell-tale odour of grease and oil that characterizes many industrial heritage sites or museums containing planes, trains and military vehicles. There are, however, smells missing. You cannot smell the sewage that was pumped through the station and away into the countryside. But another smell that is no longer detectable is the fumes of the massive boilers heated by coal (and from the early twentieth century onwards rubbish from the streets of Cambridge) which helped to power the machines which would have run twenty-four hours a day, seven days a week, from when they were installed in 1894 to their decommissioning in 1968. For environmental reasons, the museum chooses not to run the engines and they sit unused. For those visiting heritage sites that run industrial machinery, steam-trains and other machines that use fossil fuels, the smell is a key part of the experience. One solution is to turn to new eco-fuels, which provide the same ambience and smell as coal-powered steam without their negative effects. For example, the Bure Valley Railway in Norfolk has recently trialled the 'Homefire Ecoal50' fuel, which if found gave the right olfactory effect for visitors.[78] However, whilst these fuels have *less* of an environmental impact, they still have some environmental impact.

A whole series of processes from conservation or decay to re-use, recycling and adaption have altered the odours of material objects and spaces over time. These are themselves olfactory archives of historical processes that, as the following chapter suggests, we can read using interdisciplinary techniques. However, another approach is to re-odorize those spaces and objects. If we are to explore the olfactory affordances of the material archive, then it makes sense for us to think about how we might use odours with minimal danger and harm – to both ourselves and our environment. Using olfactory facsimiles developed with synthetic molecules – which often come without the dangerous health or environmental effects found in the original material – offers us a way of re-odorizing the archive and thereby helping us to understand the sensory affordances of spaces and objects.

---

[78] Michael Holden, 'Norfolk's Bure Valley Railway tests new bio-coal for steam locomotives', *Rail Advent*, 15th June 2021, https://www.railadvent.co.uk/2021/06/norfolks-bure-valley-railway-tests-new-bio-coal-for-steam-locomotives.html [accessed 01/03/2022].

Making politics sensible

Smell has a radical potential for changing how we perform our research. However, it also transforms how we communicate our conclusions to the public and to other researchers.

In Liverpool, during the 1860s concerns were raised about the importation and refining of Canadian petroleum. The high concentration of sulphur in this particular substance resulted in an offensive onion-like smell that pervaded parts of the town. Liverpool's inhabitants reacted with petitions. When this failed, they deployed olfactory protest. In order to demonstrate just how offensive the smell was, protestors broke a jar of the petroleum in front of the town hall and released the stench into its environs. By getting up the noses of councillors, they finally gained their ears.[79] Another, perhaps more famous, example comes from the Great Stink of London in the summer of 1858. Massive urban expansion coupled with institutional inertia and bickering had allowed the Thames, polluted by a mix of industrial and human waste, to turn into an open sewer. The stench that emerged from the river in the heat of July and August 1858 caused politicians and sanitarians to devise a solution to the river's parlous state: 'in times of crisis, smell trumped politics'.[80]

In both of these examples, smell convinced people of the need for political change in a way that words could not. Across the humanities an argument is being advanced that the study of the past matters for understanding pollution – and the climate and ecological crises attendant on it – and that we also have a role in encouraging solidarity and empathy, highlighting the causes and effects of environmental change, and convincing policymakers to enact evidence-based measures to ensure a sustainable future.[81] In recent years, those who study the past have worried about how to grab the attention of politicians and publics. One solution has been a call to turn to 'one screen … "shock and

---

[79] Robert G. Armstrong, 'The Smell of Air Pollution: Olfactory Senses and the Odour of Canadian Oil, 1858–1885', *Ontario History*, 112:2 (2020), pp. 211–29.
[80] David Barnes, 'Confronting Sensory Crisis in the Great Stinks of London and Paris', in William A. Cohen and Ryan Johnson (eds.), *Filth, Dirt, Disgust and Modern Life* (Minneapolis: University of Minnesota Press, 2004), p. 107.
[81] See for example the statement by 'Historians for Future', https://historiansforfuture.org/statement/ [accessed 25/01/2022]; Mark Leven, Penny Roberts and Rob Johnson (eds.), *History at the End of the World? History, Climate Change and the Possibility of Closure* (London: HEB Humanities ebooks, 2010).

awe visualisations'" of data of the sort mounted by economists.[82] But we need something more radical than – or at least in addition to – the representational tools long-wielded by quantitative scholars. We need something that is closer to the increasingly interspecies disposition of humanities disciplines that emphasizes individual and communal experience rather than hiding it in anonymizing statistics.

The contemporary challenges that humanities scholars speak to often take the form of 'hyperobjects': things that are so spatially vast or temporally extensive that they exceed the boundaries of conventional sensing.[83] Scholars interested in the past often deal with abstract structures and processes that also have this quality: power offers one such example. But we know about the cumulative actions that contribute to these processes and their outcomes through the sensorial effects they produce in the world. To quote one nineteenth-century aphorism:

> power in itself is an abstraction. We can never see it, we cannot hear it, we cannot feel it, we cannot taste it, we cannot smell it. We witness its results every-where ... All forms of power in themselves are equally invisible; power is alone known in its agents and results.[84]

Smell provides an alternative way into tracing, unveiling and then communicating the *impact* of these kinds of entities. Creative practice offers good examples here: olfactory artists such as Peter de Cupere, Anika Yi, Teresa Margolles and Michael Pinksy have all deployed odours in order to make potent and pungent points about inequality, pollution and environmental change.[85] As we work more with our noses, humanities scholars can and should borrow from creative practice in rethinking how we communicate our research in impactful and transformative ways. In using smell in our research, we may only be staging the past, but it is exactly that 'staged' property that is so powerful in lifting people out of their existing sensory habits or surroundings

---

[82] Jo Guldi and David Armitage, *The History Manifesto* (Cambridge: Cambridge University Press, 2014), p. 122.

[83] Timothy Morton, *Hyperobjects: Philosophy and Ecology after the End of the World* (Minneapolis: University of Minnesota Press, 2013).

[84] John Bate, *Six Thousand Illustrations of Moral and Religious Truths* (London: Jarrold & Sons, 1885), p. 670.

[85] For many examples, including those mentioned, see the essays in Gwenn-Ael Lynn and Debra Riley Parr (eds.), *Olfactory Art and the Political in an Age of Resistance* (London: Routledge, 2021).

in order to question the olfactory and atmospheric politics in which they are interpolated on a daily basis.

The work of olfactory artists suggests that, contrary to the suggestions of some scholars, when it comes to the olfactory past 'relevance' and 'impact' need not be seen as dirty words that always signal a 'corporatist-informed' or 'consumer-driven' approach to history.[86] Arguments about the absolute un-reachability of past ways of feeling are built on a traditional historical understanding of time in which the past is understood as distant and absent.[87] Taking smell seriously as a route into the understanding of the past and as a way of communicating our findings involves complicating our notion of the past. It involves emphasizing the irrevocable, haunting, presence of the past in the present and the ways in which smell can be used to make those ghostly sensations and atmospheres tangible.

Epistemicides

I want to finish this chapter with the suggestion that the need to re-integrate the senses into historical practice is part of a broadening and opening out of the historical discipline – indeed the humanities – and their areas of interest, methods and ways of presenting arguments to others. This broader opening out has become particularly important in the present moment, as historians grapple in ever more public ways with the need to address the historical and contemporary impact of inequity and inequality within academic disciplines, universities and wider society. In his book *The End of Cognitive Empire*, Boaventura de Sousa Santos discusses how modern Western academic traditions of knowledge production have, since the nineteenth century, 'conceived of the senses as necessary evils, indispensable but treacherous vehicles to be sorted out or unmasked'.[88] The same period that saw the emergence of academic disciplines in the West also saw attempts to match hierarchies of the senses to racial and cultural hierarchies. From Aristotle to the present philosophers,

---

[86] Mark M. Smith, *A Sensory History Manifesto* (University Park: Penn State University Press, 2021), p. 82.
[87] Berber Bevernage, *History, Memory and State-Sponsored Violence: Time and Justice* (London: Routledge, 2011), p. 108.
[88] Boaventura de Sousa Santos, *The End of the Cognitive Empire: The Coming of Age of Epistemologies of the South* (Durnham, NC: Duke University Press, 2018), p. 166.

medics, and cultural critics have placed the senses into hierarchies – ordering them in terms of their utility, objectivity and stability. What was new in the nineteenth century was their highly explicit mapping onto racist hierarchies. Perhaps the best known – the tip of the iceberg – is Lorenz Oken's mapping of humankind in his 1847 *Elements of Physiophilosophy*. In that work, Oken gave the following hierarchy:

1. The Skin-Man is the Black, African.
2. The Tongue-" is the Brown, Australian-Malayan.
3. The Nose-" is the Red, American.
4. The Ear-" is the Yellow, Asiatic-Mongolian.
5. The Eye-" is the White, European.[89]

This dismissal of certain ways of knowing the world – especially those beyond hearing and seeing – has been described by Santos as a form of 'epistemicide'. As Andrew Kettler's work on olfaction and the early modern Atlantic has shown, this process of devaluation had already started in the sixteenth and seventeenth centuries. Europeans in North America consistently emphasized the sagacious sensitivity possessed by indigenous noses. On the peripheries of empire French Jesuits and Anglo-American naturalists both used their noses and the olfactory knowledge of Native Americans to seek out sustenance and saleable commodities. Yet in the European metropole this olfactory knowledge was de-emphasized in visual tabulations of botanical knowledge or treated with a degree of suspicion.[90]

This devaluation of knowledge was deeply entwined with the workings and justification of European colonial power. In his 1709 *Voyage to Carolina*, John Lawson made the link between epistemicide and epidemics in an anecdote about two Santee men who lost their noses – possibly to syphilis – and claimed that they had willingly traded them with the 'Great Being' for 'Capacities equal with the white People in making Guns, Ammunition, &c'.[91] In this self-congratulatory

---

[89] Lorenz Oken, *Elements of Physiophilosophy* (London: Ray Society, 1847), p. 651.
[90] Andrew Kettler, '"Ravishing Odors of Paradise": Jesuits, Olfaction, and Seventeenth-century North America', *Journal of American Studies*, 50:4 (2016), pp. 827–52; Andrew Kettler, 'Delightful a Fragrance: Native American Olfactory Aesthetics within the Eighteenth-Century Anglo American Botanical Community', in Daniela Hacke and Paul Musselwhite (eds.), *Empire of the Senses: Sensory Practices of Colonialism in Early America* (Leiden: Brill, 2018), pp. 223–54.
[91] John Lawson, *A Voyage to Carolina* (London, 1709), p. 20.

anecdote about Western technological superiority and Indian credulity native *nasal* aptitude was replaced by *looking* down the barrel of a musket.

In an attempt to confront and undo the long-term consequences of this process – to decolonize the cognitive empire – the practice of research that Santos advocates centres on an openness and engagement with diverse ways of sensing and knowing, rather than forcing their translation into the pre-existing epistemologies of Western academic practice. I would not want to claim that any of the ideas that I set out in this book would immediately achieve that aim. After all, much of what I have said and will say really depends on borrowing, recycling or engaging with the tools of pre-existing academic disciplines or professional expertise. However, I think an openness to incorporating smell and other senses into our research practice will help us, at the very least, to figure out how we engage with the kinds of ideas that Santos describes. It enables us to re-engage with lost ways of using the nose, using our bodies to engage with past habits of sensing that have been effaced in an archive shot through with the powerful combined influences of colonialism and capitalism. Using our noses will help produce a more creative, interdisciplinary and inclusive form of historical practice.

Earlier on in this chapter we discussed the 'distribution of the sensible', which refers to the shaping, defining and disciplining of what can legitimately be sensed and what perceptions can be taken seriously. Engaging with smell in our research practice involves taking notice of different odours beyond those that are explicitly invoked in texts or presented to us by objects and taking seriously ways of smelling beyond our own or those of the dominant olfactory logic of archival sources. Deploying smell in museums or as a way of communicating our research to publics and policymakers works through the same methods. In both cases – that of research practice and of then presenting our findings – deploying smell involves an attempt to redistribute the sensible.[92] The goal is an expansion of the possibilities of *what* can be smelled, the *ways* in which those things can be smelled, and the discursive space in which we are able to debate and *articulate* those odours and acts of smelling.

---

[92] For an example of such a redistribution in a museum context, see Divya P. Tolia-Kelly, 'Rancière and the Re-distribution of the Sensible: The Artist Rosanna Raymond, Dissensus and Postcolonial Sensibilities within the Spaces of the Museum', *Progress in Human Geography*, 43:1 (2019), pp. 123–40.

2

Archives

Is it possible to archive smells and to use the nose in engaging with the archive? It is often taken for granted that smells and acts of smelling are characterized by 'inherent ephemerality and flux'.[1] Historical studies of smell have tended to reaffirm smell's reputation on this score. We can certainly find references in the archive to the ephemerality of scent and its perception. In 1798, Immanuel Kant, one of the enlightenment's fiercest critics of the nose, argued that 'the pleasure coming from the sense of smell is always fleeting and transient'.[2] The idea that smells and smelling are unstable and fleeting has also posed difficulties for contemporary scholars who have pointed to intransigence in the face of attempts at archival cataloguing and historicisation.[3] Smell's supposed resistance to recording in language, images and archives would suggest that it is temporally and materially ephemeral.

However, if we step back in time to the seventeenth century, texts ranging from Shakespearian sonnets to the records of scientific experimentation show considerable interest in just how long smells could last. Take, for example, Shakespeare's fifth sonnet which reflects on the preservation of scent through distillation. This act turns summer flowers into a 'liquid prisoner pent in walls of glass' and

> ... though they with winter meet,
> Leese but their show; their substance still lives sweet.[4]

---

[1] Jim Drobnick, 'Preface', in Jim Drobnick (ed.), *The Smell Culture Reader* (Oxford: Berg, 2006), p. 260; Jonathan Reinarz, *Past Scents: Historical Perspectives on Smell Scents* (Chicago: University of Illinois Press, 2014), p. 4.
[2] Immanuel Kant, *Anthropology from a Pragmatic Point of View*, ed. Robert B. Louden and Manfred Kuehn (Cambridge: Cambridge University Press, 2006), pp. 50–1.
[3] Holly Dugan, *The Ephemeral History of Perfume: Scent and Sense in Early Modern England* (Baltimore: Johns Hopkins University Press, 2011).
[4] William Shakespeare, 'Sonnet 5', in Colin Burrow (ed.), *William Shakespeare: The Complete Sonnets and Poems* (Oxford: Oxford University Press, 2002), p. 138.

Here, scent survived where summer beauty could not and distillation – as so often in discussions of smell – becomes analogous to the longer preservation of the inner essence of things. Shakespeare was not alone. In the early modern period natural histories, medical texts and philosophical treatises all wondered at the long-lasting and materially expansive qualities of odour. Civet and musk were oft-cited examples, both making it clear that perfume was anything but ephemeral. Civet was a popular early modern perfume. It was obtained from the perennial gland, close to the anus, of a cat native to parts of Africa and Asia. Materially, it was a brown, unctuous, material that had a scent bordering on the faecal. Musk was obtained from the musk deer and imported to Europe in the form of congealed sacks. These scents tickled the noses and minds of natural philosophers into attempting to mathematically calculate the surprising geographical diffusion and temporal durability of smells.[5] Civet and musk lasted a long time, lost little weight despite their atmospheric impact and thus continued to serve their original purpose long beyond their first use. In contradistinction to contemporary claims for smell's ephemerality, early modern writers were just as interested in its durability across time.

This book has partly been inspired by other work that has sought to challenge the stereotypes associated with the 'five senses'. Jonathan Sterne has criticized the tendency in historical studies of sound to fall back on an 'audio-visual' litany, composed of stereotyped differences between sound and vision. For example, this includes the oft-repeated claims that hearing is immersive while vision offers perspective or that hearing is about affect and vision is about intellect.[6] If we were to advance a similar 'olfactory-visual litany', it would include the claim that whilst smelling is fleeting, momentary and beyond capture, things that we can see are more likely to be constant, durable and easily archivable. Yet have odours and smelling ever been any more or less ephemeral than other stimuli or perceptual acts? Take, for example, a turn of phrase from an eighteenth-century satirical pamphlet in which the author defined ephemera as that 'which signifies a ting, of short life, not exceeding a day, for all the world like the false light of the snuff of a candle, which go's off

---

[5] John Keill, *An Introduction to Natural Philosophy* (London: J. Senex, 1726), p. 48; Bernard Nieuwentyt, *The Religious Philosopher*, trans. John Chamberlayne (London: J. Senex, 1719), p. 869.

[6] Jonathan Sterne, *The Audible Past: Cultural Origins of Sound Reproduction* (Durham, NC: Duke University Press, 2003), pp. 14–15.

quickly, and often leaves a cursed stink behind it'.[7] Here light is a species of momentary ephemera, but smell lingers on in the dark.

Smell's material volatility has made the possibility of archiving it difficult. Each part of the process of collecting, storing and accessing archived scents can be highly problematic. This has leant further credence to the idea that smell is ephemeral, which has in turn foreclosed many attempts to archive it. The supposed ephemerality of smell thus becomes a self-fulfilling prophecy. Yet there are in fact both intentional and unintentional archives of smell. Two issues have led to historically minded scholars ignoring these archives. On the one hand, these archives tend not to be the sort of archives that humanists work with. On the other hand, humanists have been unwilling or unable to deploy the methods that can make sense of them.

Falstaff's nose

In 1889, the Englishman, professor of English Literature, and former professor of History at McGill University in Montreal, Charles Ebenezer Moyse published a play. It bore the title *Shakespeare's Skull and Falstaff's Nose: A Fancy in Three Acts* and it was printed in London under the pseudonym Belgrave Titmarsh.[8] This latter fact was just as well, since it was a pointed satire on academic fanaticism and the obsession with authenticity that characterized late-nineteenth-century Shakespearean scholarship. One of the key elements of the plot concerns a character known only as '2nd Gentleman'. Desiring to be a 'True Shakespearean', 2nd Gentleman fixated on Falstaff's nose as the secret key to all of Shakespeare's fiction. He noted that Falstaff – a character who reappears in several of Shakespeare's plays – often uses his nose as a judge of character. In particular, 2nd Gentleman focuses on a moment in 'The Merry Wives of Windsor' when Falstaff described the scent of a fashionable perfumed gentlemen as 'smelling like Bucklersbury in simpling-time'.[9]

---

[7] Tedy O'Fogherty, *A Letter from the Revd. Faether [sic] Tedy O'Fogherty to a Count of Milan* (Dublin, 1764), p. 4.
[8] Belgrave Titmarsh [Charles Ebenezer Moyse], *Shakspere's Skull and Falstaff's Nose: A Fancy in Three Acts* (London: E. Stock, 1889).
[9] Giorgio Melchiori (ed.), *The Merry Wives of Windsor* (London: Bloomsbury, 1999), p. 217.

Since the sixteenth century Bucklersbury, a small street at the junction of Cheapside and the Poultry in the City of London, had been a centre for the trade in drugs and perfumes. The scent was such that one early-seventeenth-century pamphlet referred to a man who, 'passing through Bucklersbury, fell into a kind of trance, with the sweete smels of that street'.[10] By the eighteenth century claims were also circulating that during periods of plague Bucklersbury had always been protected from infection by the atmosphere of strong smells emanating from apothecary's and perfumer's shops.[11] Despite evidence of eighteenth-century complaints about the stink from overflowing cellars and night-soil in the street, Bucklersbury seems to have maintained its fragrant reputation and leases show that druggists and chemists inhabited the street well into the nineteenth century.[12]

By this point Bucklersbury's scent lingered on in texts on perfume practice. The street became part of the history and heritage of perfumery, as men such as Eugene Rimmel attempted to claim the status of 'art' and 'profession' for perfumery.[13] In the early modern period the sweet smells of Bucklersbury had been constituted by a particular way of smelling and a nexus of olfactory skills that united apothecaries and perfumers together. By the second half of the nineteenth century, when Rimmel was writing, shifts in medical understanding and pharmaceutical marketing meant that the apothecary and the perfumer were no longer united in the way that they had been in the sixteenth and seventeenth centuries. Smells no longer communicated medicinal power. The flavour and smell of medicine became something to cover up or eradicate rather than an integral part of how medicines worked.[14] By the late nineteenth century, both the smellscape and a particular way of perceiving it had disappeared.

For 2nd Gentleman, Bucklersbury provided the key to understanding the sensitivity of Falstaff's nose and thereby comprehending the significance of

---

[10] Roger Marbecke, *A Defence of Tabacco with a Friendly Answer to the Late Printed Booke Called Worke for Chimny-Sweepers, & c* (London: Richard Field, 1602).

[11] Authors seemed to have principally taken this from republished editions of Thomas Moffett's sixteenth-century text, Thomas Moffett, *Health's Improvement* (London: T. Osborne, 1743), p. xiii; Londinensis, 'Observations on Pennant's London', *The Gentleman's Magazine*, 68 (1790), p. 612.

[12] City of London Commission of Sewers Journal, 1752, London Metropolitan Archives, London, CLA/006/AD/03/016; Deeds and Papers Relating to Corbyn and Co., Chemists and Druggists, 1726–1891, Wellcome Library, London, MS.5435.

[13] Eugene Rimmel, *The Book of Perfumes* (London: Chapman & Hall, 1865), p. 206; C. J. S. Thompson, *The Mystery and Lure of Perfume* (London: John Lane, 1927), p. 90.

[14] William Tullett, *Smell in Eighteenth-century England: A Social Sense* (Oxford: Oxford University Press, 2019), pp. 88–105; Erica M. Storm, 'Gilding the Pill: The Sensuous Consumption of Patent Medicines, 1815–1841', *Social History of Medicine*, 31:1 (2018), pp. 41–60.

Shakespeare's whole oeuvre. He wrote a 910-page monograph on the matter and presented his results to a society of 'True Shakespeareans'. In outlining his findings, 2nd Gentleman also discussed his method at length:

> My investigation accordingly resolved itself into the following heads: (a) The size of Bucklersbury; (b) the sanitary, or rather the unsanitary condition of Bucklersbury relative to the other districts of London; (c) a description of the nature and potency of the evil odours which abounded in Bucklersbury, and consequently the amount of resistance, expressed mathematically, which perfumes would meet with from those odours; (d) the prevailing perfumes of Bucklersbury; (e) the last and most knotty question of all – the average condition of the air at what I may call the average spot, namely along the medial line of a street of average width.[15]

To aid his research, the gentleman sought a late-nineteenth-century city that approached the sanitary conditions of 'London in Shakspere's day' and settled on Cologne, no doubt inspired by the poet Samuel Taylor Coleridge's earlier identification of the German town's 'two and seventy stenches'.[16] After reading a series of obscure texts, the gentleman also made

> many physical and chemical experiments, even to the determination of the formula of the perfume in the average air in the average spot, namely, along the medial line of a street of average width, and can give you incontestable evidence of the degree of sensibility which I imagine Falstaff's nose to have possessed, by allowing the average air of the Shakspearian Bucklersbury, contained in this vial, to escape into the hall.[17]

Having finished his explanation, he uncorked the vial and a 'general sniffing' on the part of the gathered Shakespearians ensued.

The target for this satire is clear. Moyes was poking fun at the attempts by scholars such as Frederick James Furnivall to assay the authorship of Shakespeare's plays through forms of 'scientific' philological analysis.[18] However, by referring to chemistry Moyes was particularly pointing to the work

---

[15] Titmarsh, *Shakspere's Skull*, p. 44.
[16] Samuel Taylor Coleridge, *The Works of Samuel Taylor Coleridge, Prose and Verse* (Philadelphia: Thomas Cowperthwait & Co., 1840), p. 228.
[17] Titmarsh, *Shakspere's Skull*, p. 46.
[18] Laurie E. Maguire, *Shakespearean Suspect Texts: The 'Bad' Quartos and Their Contexts* (Cambridge: Cambridge University Press, 1996), p. 62.

of Furnivall's colleague, Frederick Gard Fleay. Fleay went even further than Furnivall in his quest for a scientifically provable provenance for Shakespeare's plays. He suggested that tests on texts could be drawn up in the 'same form as chemical tables for the laboratory' and argued that Shakespearean critics required 'thorough training in the Natural Sciences, especially in Mineralogy, Classificatory Botany, and above all, in Chemical Analysis'.[19] It has been noted that Fleay and Furnivall's visions of mass-quantitative analysis of text do not seem so far removed from the computational analysis of texts common in the digital humanities today.[20] But for late-nineteenth-century readers, the wearying extent of 2nd Gentleman's investigations and his use of chemical methods would have put him squarely in Fleay's – quite lonely – corner.

The odours of this Shakespearean satire might well set off a feeling of Proustian recognition and recollection among scholars today. Elements of 2nd Gentleman's method sail remarkably close to past, current and even future possible ways of accessing, understanding and narrating the odours of the past.

By initially attending to the 'sanitary, or rather unsanitary condition' of London and its streets, our Shakespearian scholar was evoking a long-running tendency to associate unsanitary stench with simpler, earlier, geographically or socially other, and therefore less civilized societies.[21] Both popular and academic history in the late nineteenth and twentieth centuries often referred to smell in terms that associated stench with an earlier age. In 1919, the American scholar James Harvey Robinson, a purveyor of the 'New History' that linked the historical and social sciences in the aid of social improvement, described how in eighteenth-century Paris 'the filth and the bad smells of former times still remained'.[22] In another of Robinson's works, it is telling that a passage labelled in the margin 'towns still medieval in the eighteenth century' described how the 'disgusting odors even in the best quarters ... offered a marked contrast to the European cities of to-day, which have grown tremendously in the last hundred years in size, beauty, and comfort'.[23] In 1947 Joan Evans, the

---

[19] Frederick Gard Fleay, *Shakespeare Manual* (London: Macmillan & Co., 1876), pp. 108, 242.
[20] James Turner, *Philology: The Forgotten Origins of the Modern Humanities* (Oxford: Princeton University Press, 2014), p. 263.
[21] Mark Jenner, 'Follow Your Nose? Smell, Smelling, and Their Histories', *The American Historical Review*, 116:2 (2011), pp. 339–40.
[22] James Harvey Robinson, *Medieval and Modern Times* (Boston: Ginn, 1916), p. 446.
[23] James Harvey Robinson, Charles A. Beard and James Henry Breasted, *Outlines of European History* (Bostin: Ginn, 2, 1914), ii, p. 123.

English art historian, described how on wandering around early-nineteenth-century French capital one might encounter 'muddy little streets that still recalled medieval Paris: evil – smelling little streets'.[24] For late-nineteenth and twentieth-century historians the term 'medieval' communicated ill-smelling and unsanitary cities.

2nd Gentleman was also not alone in contrasting an odorous and therefore imperfect European continent with the clean and pleasant land of England. In 1893, the literary critic and historian Walter Besant described a medieval London mired in stench, but added:

> The medieval smell, the smell of great towns, has left London, but in old towns of the Continent, as in the old streets of Brussels, it meets and greets us to the present day. Breathing this air with difficulty, and perhaps with nausea, you may say, 'Such and such was the air in which the citizens of London delighted when Edward III was King.'[25]

As Besant and 2nd Gentleman suggest, to travel to foreign shores was to meet with the smell of England's past. In early-twentieth-century travel writing 'medieval' was often used as an olfactory descriptor. In the 1930s Grace Murphey described the Jewish Ghettos of Polish cities that she visited as 'smelly – an ancient, medieval odor', while John Otway Percy Bland noted in 1921 that 'in the matter of smells and squalor' Peking was still 'a very medieval spot'.[26] Historians and travel writers were making the same rhetorical move. In both genres, the precise smell of towns and cities in the medieval or early modern periods did not matter. What smell did in these texts was to create a sense of 'past-ness'. They evoked a less sanitized and therefore less civilized world.

By painting the history of smell as a battle between 'evil odours' and 'perfume' 2nd Gentleman also gestured to two further characteristics that are common in historical and contemporary histories of smell: a tendency to map

---

[24] Joan Evans, *The Unselfish Egoist: A Life of Joseph Joubert* (London: Longmann, 1947), p. 131.
[25] Walter Besant, *London: After the Romans. Saxon and Norman. Plantagenet* (London: Heinemann and Balestier, 1893), p. 243.
[26] Grace Humphrey, *Poland, the Unexplored* (Indianapolis: The Bobbs-Merrill Company, 1931), p. 273; John Otway Percy Bland, *China, Japan, Korea* (London: C. Scribner Sons, 1921), p. 286. Humphrey was not alone in associating the smell of Jewish ghettos with a mediaeval past. In his 1915 biography of St Catherine of Siena Johannes Jørgensen noted that 'those who at the present day walk through the narrow, dark and ill-smelling streets in the Ghetto of Siena, can obtain a faint impression of the horrors that the cities of the Middle Ages offered to the senses', see Johanness Jøgensen, *Saint Catherine of Siena* (London: Longman, 1938).

the culture of scent onto a binary of 'foul' and 'fragrant' and a concomitant attempt to paint the history of smell as dialectical struggle between the two ends of that binary.[27] This also points to the dominant place of two particular professions – the sanitarian and the perfumer – in histories of smell. The desire to re-create the 'average air' in the 'average spot' in a street of 'average width' also points to a fantasy of historical compression: a desire, common to some approaches to smell, to distil 'the' smell of a time or place into a single vial of scent, a paragraph or a static map.[28] Finally, the end goal of the gentleman's research, assessing the sensitivity of Falstaff's nose, is reached by analysing the smells of Bucklersbury itself. This points to the tension implicit in the history of smell between the histories of smells and histories of smelling, between understanding the olfactory environment and the way in which people perceived it.[29]

Yet 2nd Gentleman's approach also gestures to the possibilities of interdisciplinary collaboration that can move us beyond simple binaries or attempts to distil the aromatic zeitgeist of a period. The attempt to physically map a historical space and the circulation of odours within it does not seem so far from current attempts to digitally model the soundscapes of earlier eras.[30] This has borrowed on the modern science of acoustics, which has – especially since the early twentieth century – attempted to make buildings sound better. The twentieth century has also seen the development of an odour regulation industry, which has attempted to make our environments smell less offensive. This industry has developed its own techniques which are comparable to acoustic modelling, in which the possible temporal and geographical reach of smells is mapped in both analogue and digital forms. In the future we

---

[27] Reinarz, *Past Scents*, p. 210; Clare Brant, 'Fume and Perfume: Some Eighteenth-Century Uses of Smell', *Journal of British Studies*, 43:4 (2004), pp. 445–6.

[28] For a premier example of this fantasy of distillation, see the recreation of the 'Pong de Paris' in the documentary series 'Filthy Cities' (BBC, 2011) presented by Dan Snow, https://www.bbc.co.uk/programmes/p00g4k6c#:~:text=Just%20200%20years%20ago%2C%20Paris,and%20smelliest%20cities%20in%20Europe [accessed 25/08/2022].

[29] A tension apparent in Mark Jenner, 'Tasting Lichfield, Touching China: Sir John Floyer's Senses', *The Historical Journal*, 53:3 (2010), pp. 669–70.

[30] For examples see John N. Wall, 'Transforming the Object of Our Study: The Early Modern Sermon and the Virtual Paul's Cross Project', *Journal of Digital Humanities*, 3:1 (2014), http://journalofdigitalhumanities.org/3-1/transforming-the-object-of-our-study-by-john-n-wall/ [accessed 07/03/2022]; Catriona Cooper, 'The Sounds of Debate in Georgian England: Auralising the House of Commons', *Parliamentary History*, 38:1 (2019), pp. 60–73.

might deploy odour dispersion modelling to historical topographical and architectural sources to model the dispersal of smell in historical space.[31] Such experiments have already been tried at a more analogue level, analysing how long perfume used in a Jacobean play performed in the recreated Blackfriars theatre would take to get to different parts of the audience in order to ascertain how scent related to the speech and movement on stage.[32] 2nd Gentleman's use of 'chemical experiments' also points towards the gains that historians can achieve by working more closely with heritage scientists, using analytical chemistry to extract the historical odours of places and objects.[33] These techniques offer historians of smell new tools that have yet to be widely applied but may help shape the future of the field.

Built heritage and the landscape around us offer us a kind of implicit and explicit olfactory archive. Both feeding smells back into historical spaces and extracting smells from them can allow us to use the historic environment as an archive of scent. As the Blackfriars theatre example suggests, surviving historical spaces and landscapes offer us opportunities to track atmospheric affordances for the distribution of odours. Taking an example from studies of theatre is particularly apt for the argument being advanced here. Histories of the body, emotions and the senses are used to thinking of feeling as a kind of 'performance', a 'doing that transforms the subject in myriad ways'.[34] Yet such accounts tend to emphasize the actor and the illocutionary force of their script rather than the stage on which the performance plays out. Performances take place in space and place and their olfactory atmospheres often play a role in their interpretation – whether they are explicitly mentioned in textual accounts or not. As the history of smell's use in a theatrical context – a phenomenon that stretches back to ancient drama – suggests, the relationship

---

[31] This is something that the author is interested in pursuing; for work on odour dispersion see Cecilia Conti et al., 'Measurements Techniques and Models to Assess Odor Annoyance: A Review', *Environment International*, 134 (2020), p. 105461.

[32] Holly Crawford Pickett, 'The Idolatrous Nose: Incense on the Early Modern Stage', in Jane Hwang Degenhardt and Elizabeth Williamson (eds.), *Religion and Drama in Early Modern England* (Farnham: Ashgate, 2011), pp. 35–6.

[33] For an introduction to this approach, see Cecilia Bembibre and Matija Strlič, 'Smell of Heritage: A Framework for the Identification, Analysis and Archival of Historic Odours', *Heritage Science*, 5:2 (2017), pp. 1–11.

[34] Dolores Martin-Moruno and Beatriz Pichel, 'Introduction', in Dolores Martin-Moruno and Beatriz Pichel (eds.), *Emotional Bodies: The Historical Performativity of Emotions* (Chicago: University of Illinois Press, 2019), p. 11.

between smell, nose and space offers up plenty of potential for mixed messages and unintended responses. Experimental archaeology is already pursuing simple technological solutions that allow us to re-odorize heritage landscapes and buildings. This includes the 'Dead Man's Nose' – a simple prototype-augmented reality device that can be worn around the neck and programmed to release different scents that may have been present at different geographical locations in a walk through a historical site. This has been used to release different smells within different parts of Hougoumont Farm – a significant site within the broader battle that took place in 1815 at Waterloo – that would have been linked to different points in the battle including the day before, the day of, the day immediately after and later in the year when the farm returned to its former use. These kinds of tools allow a re-odorizing of a historical landscape that now exists as bucolic, calm, fields: 'by being directly assaulted with the acrid smell of battle, burning buildings and human anguish, some of that landscape's hidden history is revealed'.[35] These scents operate as a challenge to us to think differently about historical sites by revealing the lost monumentality of smell.

Bodies can be thought of in the same way as environments. We often associate smell with memory. But smell is not just mnemonic but habitual. The two are distinct: 'memory is an image of the past, habit is the past's repetition in the present'.[36] You, the contemporary reader, and historical actors were formed by habits. As individuals today and in the past have carved paths through environments that provide particular sensory affordances, so those environments have carved paths within our bodies creating a bank of habits for parsing our future sensory interactions. These habitual affordances may influence experience in ways that are not always recognized by us or represented in texts or images by historical actors. The implicit olfactory archive beyond the text – historical landscapes and buildings, reconstructions and re-enactments, the smellscapes around us every day – provides a resource for imagining these kinds of deposits.

However, despite its creative and – to this author – intellectual stimulating ideas about olfactory research methodology, Moyse's play was a satire, and the

---

[35] Stuart Eve, 'A Dead Man's Nose: Using Smell to Explore the Battlefield of Waterloo', in Victoria Henshaw et al. (eds.), *Designing with Smell: Practices, Techniques, and Challenges* (London: Routledge, 2018), pp. 211–18.

[36] Clare Carlisle, *On Habit* (London: Routledge, 2014), p. 25.

fact that 2nd Gentleman's methods were *not* taken seriously at the time or (in many quarters) today is partly the consequence of ideas about smell, academic disciplinary conventions and historiographical trends that also have their roots in the nineteenth century. Many of these disciplinary qualms still inform how we see smell today. Simply put, Moyse's satire worked because academic humanities disciplines that emerged in the nineteenth century – especially history – were overwhelmingly textual, documentary, disciplines.

Leopold von Ranke, the German historian so often credited with developing modern academic history in the nineteenth century, emphasized again and again that history was about *reading* the documents – preferably as many as possible. We can summarize the bent of late-nineteenth- and early-twentieth-century historical research in the terms offered by two French historians in an 1898 textbook for trainee historians: 'History is done with documents … Lacking documents, the history of immense periods of the past of humankind is forever unknowable. For nothing can replace documents: no documents, no history.'[37] History has subsequently moved beyond a concern with purely textual sources. We now use visual, material and auditory culture in our work. However, with a few exceptions in certain areas of material culture, we still tend to engage with all of these sources through a form of interpretation in which we read material for meaning. We may read sources in different ways to nineteenth-century historians, but reading is still ultimately what historians do.

The metaphors we have used in discussing historical practice since the nineteenth century are also indicative of the visual bias of the historian's craft. When proponents of scientific academic history in the late nineteenth century decried the popular histories of their predecessors, they turned to the metaphor of taste. In 1879, John Robert Seeley accused earlier historians of producing a past that was 'adulterated with sweet, unwholesome stuff to please the popular palate.'[38] Scientific history, Seeley suggested, would provide more wholesome but less piquant fair. In his introduction to a 1909 translation of Leopold von Ranke's *History of the Latin and Teutonic Nations*, the Oxford

---

[37] Kasper Risbjerg Eskildsen, 'Leopold von Ranke's Archival Turn: Location and Evidence in Modern Historiography', *Modern Intellectual History*, 5:3 (2008), p. 451.

[38] Ian Hesketh, 'Writing History in Macaulay's Shadow: J.R. Seeley, E.A. Freeman, and the Audience for Scientific History in Late Victorian Britain', *Journal of the Canadian Historical Association*, 22:2 (2011), pp. 30–56.

historian Edward Armstrong noted that Ranke's insatiable archival appetite had led custodians to complain that he 'read with his hand, just as a recent Oxford professor was accused of judging books and examination papers by the smell rather than by the sight'.[39] Smell, taste and even touch were all used to describe forms of history in which careful reading and research were absent. An obsession with the sensorial was equated with an 'antiquarian' sensibility, a fascination with collecting authentic material remnants of the past – rather than interpreting them – that included breathing in the smells of 'mouldy air'.[40] The boundaries of History as a discipline were (and are) policed by a particular 'distribution of the sensible', the ways of sensing that are possible or acknowledged within it.[41]

In the twentieth century, a more audio-visual way of describing the archive has predominated. Social historians – who often talk of rescuing the 'voices' of the ignored or inarticulate – have frequently turned to metaphors of careful, attentive, listening. E. P. Thompson's advice was that 'the historian has got to be listening all the time … If he listens, then the material itself will begin to speak through him'.[42] The authority of the written sources is testified to by their ventriloquizing of the attentive historian as a mouthpiece for the past. The closest a historian has come to invoking smell as a metaphor for historical research is Emmanuel Le Roy Ladurie, who made a distinction between two types of historians: wide-ranging parachutists and detail-obsessed truffle-hunters. Historians frequently trot out Ladurie's distinction, equating it with a distinction between roving eyes and noses that snuff the ground. But it transpires that this is not what Ladurie had in mind: his metaphor depended on a distinction, inspired by the war in Algeria between 1954 and 1962, between parachutists roving across the earth and truffle-hunters who dug deep into it.[43] So it seems fair to say that historians have rarely used their noses and, in describing their practice, they have rarely used the metaphor of smell.

---

[39] Edward Armstrong, 'Introduction', in Leopold von Ranke (ed.), *History of the Latin and Teutonic Nations (1494–1514)*, trans. G. R. Dennis (London: George Bell and Sons, 1909), p. xiii.

[40] Stephen Bann, *The Inventions of History: Essays on the Representation of the Past* (Manchester: Manchester University Press, 1990), pp. 109–10.

[41] Jacques Rancière, *The Politics of Aesthetics* (London: Bloomsbury, 2013), p. 89.

[42] E. P. Thompson and Henry Abelove et al. (eds.), *Visions of History* (Manchester: Manchester University Press, 1976), p. 14.

[43] J. H. Elliott, *History in the Making* (London: Yale University Press, 2012), p. 197.

Volatile records

As we have already suggested, one reason for this is that since the nineteenth-century history has been – above all – an archival practice. From the eighteenth century onwards archives and libraries were often imagined (though the reality was frequently different) as spaces that shut out the noise, smells and dust of the street whilst letting in plenty of light for looking.[44] Laments about the 'unbearable smell' of eighteenth-century archives led to calls for better ventilation.[45] Early practices of conservation did not help. In the 1820s Wilhelm Grimm was working on palimpsest manuscripts at the library of the University of Göttingen – home to the scholars that influenced Ranke and the emergence of modern academic history – using liver of sulphur tinctures to try and reveal hidden text. One unfortunate side effect of this process was the production of hydrogen sulphide, with its rotten-egg stink, and in April 1827 Grimm noted:

> The very smell of the reagent had such a strong effect that I had to give up this winter and had to wait until milder weather allowed me to work with the windows open.[46]

By the nineteenth century, archival smells were understood as a problem to be addressed by architectural intervention. In 1889, Dr Harry Campbell lamented to the *Lancet* on the 'impure' air of the British Museum's domed library and called for better ventilation. Books were particularly porous: a banquet had recently been held in 'one of our large libraries' and, despite opened windows, the 'dinner smell' lingered in the reading room for weeks after. An overly odorous atmosphere was incompatible with intellectual work: 'It is not from the poisonous exhalations of the body that the subtle essence of thought can be distilled.'[47] It should therefore not be surprising that with the

---

[44] Shannon Mattern, 'Resonant Texts: Sounds of the American Public Library', *Senses and Society*, 2:3 (2007), p. 283.
[45] Markus Friedrick, *The Birth of the Archive: A History of Knowledge* (Ann Arbor: University of Michigan Press, 2018), p. 98.
[46] Felix Albrecht, 'Between Boon and Bane: The Use of Chemical Reagents in Palimpsest Research in the Nineteenth Century', in M. J. Driscoll (ed.), *Care and Conservation of Manuscripts 13: Proceedings of the Thirteenth International Seminar Held at the University of Copenhagen 13th–15th April 2001* (Copenhagen: Museum Tusculanum Press, 2012), p. 156.
[47] Dr Harry Campbell, 'Ventilation of Libraries', *The Lancet*, 20th April 1889, p. 818.

professionalization of library and archival work in the late nineteenth century, associations identified ventilation in their buildings as a key concern.[48] References in library and archive association journals to ridding the library of 'garret-like' odours, the garret being the loft-space quarters associated with the starving poet and newspaper hack, suggested the equation of inodorous archives and intellectually significant work.[49] The desire to rid archives of distracting odours was also framed in ways that distinguished the 'proper' specialist user from the general public. For some, as for one 1920s visitor to the Sainte-Geneviève Library in Paris, the presence of the public who were 'apt to impinge rather too violently on one's sense of smell' disturbed their consultation of the collections.[50]

As this suggests, though we are apt to romanticize the smell of the library and the archive, the scent is partly constructed by keeping other people and other odours out. Ideas about personal space and hygiene practices that emerged in the eighteenth and nineteenth centuries aimed to circumscribe both the odours that were emitted by individuals in public space and the boundaries of acceptable middle- and upper-class corporeality.[51] One legacy of that process is the type of embodiment found in the library and archive. Indeed, today smell is used as one way of policing the acceptable users of public libraries and archives – rules that have reinforced exclusionary practices based around ableism, classism and racism under the guise of actions aimed at unusually odorous individuals.[52] As in museums, nineteenth- and twentieth-century archives and libraries have accumulated a series of rules that have prescribed and proscribed the correct forms of embodiment that can take place within them: they are places for, above all, inodorus and silent looking – not active

---

[48] William H. Greenhough, *On Ventilation, Heating, and Lighting of Free Public Libraries* (Reading, 1890).

[49] D. F. Lincoln, 'Ventilation of Libraries', *The Library Journal*, 4 (1879), p. 255.

[50] *Proceedings of the Annual Conference of the Pacific Northwest Library Association* (Tacoma: Big Four Inn, 1928), p. 29.

[51] Alain Corbin, *The Foul and the Fragrant* (Cambridge, MA: Harvard University Press, 1986); Tullett, *Smell in Eighteenth-century England*.

[52] Alan Hyde, *Bodies of Law* (Princeton: Princeton University Press, 1997), pp. 252–7; Nat Lazakis, '"It Is a Non-Negotiable Order": Public Libraries' Body Odor Bans and the Ableist Politics of Purity', *Journal of Radical Librarianship*, 6 (2020), pp. 24–52.

sniffing.⁵³ Smell was – now is – not the sense on which humanistic knowledge and archives have been built.

The textual bent of historical scholarship also meant that it took a long time for senses beyond vision to get into the historical archive. In the late nineteenth century, the phonograph emerged from and helped perpetuate a deep-seated fascination with the idea of listening to the voices of the dead.⁵⁴ This was part of what Kate Lacey has called the 'phonographic imagination', a set of ideas about sound that both preceded and helped inform the response to the phonograph.⁵⁵ The early twentieth century saw the construction of a whole series of sound archives. However, the encouragement for these archives did not come from history and initially they were rarely used by academic historians. Instead, anthropologists, linguists and musicologists developed archives of recorded speech and music.⁵⁶ It would only be in the later twentieth century that historians began to make use of these archives with any regularity.

Smell has been even more neglected in this respect. Perhaps the closest equivalents to the 'phonographic imagination' when it comes to smell are the processes of distillation, enfleurage and other techniques for extracting scent from objects that have been developed in perfumery and medicine across the span of history. They form part of what I would like to call the 'extractive imagination' – a set of ideas that centre on an ability to extract the essential, unique, scent of an object, body or space. This basic idea has informed a great deal of how western European culture has engaged with smell over the past 500 years – from perfumery and gas chromatography to sniffer dogs and racist stereotyping. It still informs the way historians – popular and academic – talk about smell.

However, in the late nineteenth and early twentieth centuries the 'extractive imagination' failed to lead to comparable academic archives of the sort which

---

⁵³ Constance Classen, 'Museum Manners: The Sensory Life of the Early Museum', *Journal of Social History*, 40:4 (2007), pp. 895–914.
⁵⁴ Sterne, *The Audible Past*, pp. 287–334.
⁵⁵ Britta Lange, 'Archive, Collection, Museum: On the History of the Archiving of Voices at the Sound Archive of the Humboldt University', *Journal of Sonic Studies*, 13 (2017), https://www.researchcatalogue.net/view/326465/326466/0/0 [accessed 22/03/2021].
⁵⁶ Kate Lacey, *Listening Publics: The Politics and Experience of Listening in the Media Age* (London: Polity, 2013).

the phonograph and the phonographic imagination produced. In fact, smell's late-nineteenth-century moment of modernity – its closest equivalent to the technology of the phonograph or the photograph – helped make smell seem even more evanescent and immaterial. The late nineteenth century witnessed a synthetic revolution in which chemists were able to synthesize and reproduce aromas on an industrial scale. In the same period phonographic and photographic technologies made sound and image material in the form of disks, cylinders and film. These material remediations and their – relatively at least – instantaneous processes of capture and re-play were commercially accessible and reproducible.

But the synthesis of aromas and their use in perfume took place in the laboratory and the production centres of industrial chemistry. One result of the synthetic revolution in perfume was the creation of mass market perfumery that was advertised in ever more abstract ways.[57] In the eighteenth century, perfumery had been named and advertised in the encyclopaedic language of its ingredients: lavender, rose and bergamot for example. In the late nineteenth and twentieth centuries product names and advertising imagery increasingly emphasized the spaces, emotions and identities associated with a perfume instead of the material sources of scent. The shift to synthetic scents was also matched by relative decline of perfume-making in the home, meaning that knowledge of perfume creation was less widely spread, and further mystifying the relationship between perfume and its material processes of production. It has often been suggested that the 'volatility and immateriality' of smell means that it 'inherently challenges commodification, collection, and archiving'.[58] I would suggest that the idea that smell is immaterial – and therefore difficult to archive – and subjective – and therefore unreliable as a tool in historical inquiry – owes a great deal to the legacy of this broader cultural, commercial and technological shift.

The language of smell – the fact that in English we tend to talk about it in metaphorical, encyclopaedic acts of comparison (this smells of coffee, or that smells of roses) – has also meant that it has historically been difficult to catalogue. Over the last 400 years individuals have attempted to devise

---

[57] Ann-Sophie Barwich and Matthew Rodriguez, 'Fashion Fades, Chanel No.5 Remains: Epistemology between Style and Technology', *Berichte zur Wissenschaftsgeschichte*, 43:3 (2020), pp. 367–84.
[58] Brian Goltzenleuchter, 'Scenting the Antiseptic Institution', in Victorian Henshaw et al. (eds.), *Designing with Smell: Practices, Techniques, and Challenges* (London: Routledge, 2018), p. 248.

classifications for smell, from medics and botanists in the seventeenth and eighteenth centuries to psychologists and chemists in the nineteenth and twentieth centuries. But these have involved a degree of borrowing: from materials (goaty and garlicy), other senses (sweet, bitter) or material states (putrid, burnt). This makes smell – as distinguished from the things that produce it – difficult to index and catalogue. The lack of appropriate meta-data or an organizing system for smell in the archive means that scents frequently slip between the cracks. The scents of twentieth-century experiments with smell-o-vision have often not been archived, though we can find responses to the scents in newspaper reviews and advertisements.[59]

Smell still resists archival cataloguing in the twenty-first century. The 2007 multi-media installation *La Bouche du Rois* by Romuald Hazoumé which appeared at the British Museum as part of the 200th anniversary of the abolition of slavery combined video, sound and petrol can 'masks' arranged in the shape of the *Brookes* slave ship made famous by abolitionists. But the installation also mixed the smells of tobacco, spices, urine and faeces, conveying the filth which lay at the roots of the lucre and luxury generated by slavery. Audience surveys by the consultancy Morris Hargreaves McIntyre demonstrated that the smell was one of the elements which made the most impact on visitors: the 'aromatic atmosphere was powerful' and the 'smell … was evocative'.[60] Abolitionists, slaves and others who experienced the eighteenth-century Atlantic slave trade frequently remarked on the offensive odours of both the middle passage and plantation work.[61] However, much like the original eighteenth-century engraving, with its visually tidy rows of inodorous bodies, the archiving of the installation ignored its smells. In the British Museum catalogue, it is very difficult to find any references to the smells associated with the installation, though most other elements of it have been archived.[62]

---

[59] Jennifer Jenkins, 'Archiving the Ephemeral Experience', in Karen F. Gracy (ed.), *Emerging Trends in Archival Science* (London: Rowman and Littlefield, 2018), pp. 81–2.

[60] Miranda Stearn, 'Contemporary Challenges: Artistic Interventions in Museums and Galleries Dealing with Challenging Histories', in Jenny Kidd et al. (eds.), *Challenging History in the Museum* (London: Routledge, 2016), pp. 102–4.

[61] Though racist discourse often blamed slaves themselves, imputing their odour to both culturally caused and innate filthiness, see William Tullett, 'Grease and Sweat: Race and Smell in Eighteenth-century English Culture', *Cultural and Social History*, 13:6 (2016), pp. 315–6; Andrew Kettler, *The Smell of Slavery: Olfactory Racism and the Atlantic World* (Cambridge: Cambridge University Press, 2020).

[62] See the following search in the catalogue, https://www.britishmuseum.org/collection/search?keyword=bouche&keyword=du&keyword=roi [accessed 22/02/2021].

One reason for the supposed difficulty with archiving smells or deploying the nose in historical practice is that smells are ineffable, and their description is highly culturally contingent. Smells are difficult to tie down on the page because, whilst they can be entrapped in alcohol and oils, they resist encapsulation in inky words. If we were to come up with another binary in our 'olfactory-visual litany', it would be that whilst vision has its own specific language, our vocabulary of smell is impoverished. Yet scholarship is also suggesting that the ineffability of smell is neither trans-historical nor culturally universal. From a temporal perspective, the work of historians on the early modern period has begun to pick apart the assumption that the English lexicon suffers from a lack of olfactory terms. Early modern English contained a multitude of words for smell that are now largely absent or considered archaic.[63] To some extent the narrowing of the olfactory vocabulary in the English language is not an unchanging constant but a historical process. Over the course of the eighteenth century the vocabulary of smell in English language texts shifted. Writers turned from a language of smell based in material comparison to an increasingly binary and affect-laden vocabulary of agreeable and disagreeable, pleasant and disgusting, or grateful and offensive.[64] From a geographical perspective the pioneering work of Asifa Majid has also shown that the ineffability of smell is not innate. Many languages across the globe have much more complex olfactory vocabularies than English.[65]

It is also the case that other disciplines outside of the humanities, or indeed outside of academia in general, have developed specialist ways of talking about odour that are adapted to their particular use. The perfume industry is an obvious example here. The noses that craft perfume, the market-researchers that test them on consumers and the advertisers that help sell the final scents all deploy different types of specialist vocabularies that are codified in odour wheels, lists and tables.[66] Similarly, both academics and industry specialists involved in managing the odours of water, air and waste have developed

---

[63] Dugan, *The Ephemeral History of Perfume*, p. 5.
[64] Tullett, *Smell in Eighteenth-century England*, pp. 36–8.
[65] Asifa Majid, 'Human Olfaction at the Intersection of Language, Culture, and Biology', *Trends in Cognitive Sciences*, 25:2 (2021), pp. 111–23.
[66] Fabian Muniesa and Anne-Sophie Trébuchet-Breitwiller, 'Becoming a Measuring Instrument', *Journal of Cultural Economy*, 3:3 (2010), pp. 321–37; Bruno Latour, 'How to Talk about the Body? The Normative Dimension of Science Studies', *Body & Society*, 10:2–3 (2004), pp. 205–29.

categorizations and odour wheels derived from chemical techniques and panels of human noses.⁶⁷ We can categorize these odour wheels, to quote Steven Shapin, as 'intersubjectivity engines' that are part of our modern 'aesthetic-industrial complex'.⁶⁸ These wheels take the supposedly subjective and attempt to create forms of intersubjective agreement: whilst some of them are intended to be specialist and technical, others depend on trying to stabilize an 'average' sense of smell and a normative nose. These are tools with their own histories, and those histories – for example of the development of flavour science and its commercial application – are now being written.⁶⁹

But we should consider whether historians themselves could develop specialist vocabularies of smell, odour wheels and other tools – or draw on those already available elsewhere. We can like to generate our own little intersubjectivity engines to help us in our history of odours. Heritage scientists, for example, have already developed a historic odour book wheel – based around analysis of the odorants of old books and the descriptions offered by members of the public.⁷⁰ Suggestive work has begun to explore the possibilities of an odour wheel for use in art historical contexts.⁷¹ Historians have often been willing to borrow languages from other disciplines – whether that is art history, material culture and museology, or musicology and acoustics – to help describe and analyse the characteristics of the visual, material and auditory aspects of the past. These vocabularies help them speak across disciplines about their work, and similar borrowings will allow historians of smell to do the same. They will also help us better archive and preserve smells by providing the languages that can be used in generating olfactory archival meta-data.

The idea that archives of smell are impossible is also contradicted by the fact that we can find both historical and contemporary attempts to archive scent. One such contemporary archive is the Osmothèque in Paris, which holds collections of historical and contemporary perfumes. These are stored

---

⁶⁷ Ruth M. Fisher et al., 'Framework for the Use of Odour Wheels to Manage Odours throughout Wastewater Biosolids Processing', *Science of the Total Environment,* 634 (2018), pp. 214–23; Laura Capelli et al., 'Overview of Odour Measurement Methods: The Odour Observatory as an Informative Tool for Citizen Science Based Approaches to Odour Management', *Detritus,* 12 (2020), pp. 169–75.
⁶⁸ Steven Shapin, 'The Sciences of Subjectivity', *Social Studies of Science,* 42:2 (2012), pp. 178–9.
⁶⁹ Nadia Berenstein, 'Flavor Added: The Sciences of Flavor and the Industrialization of Taste in America', PhD thesis, University of Pennsylvania, 2017.
⁷⁰ Bembibre and Strlič, 'Smell of Heritage', pp. 1–11.
⁷¹ Sofia Ehrich et al., 'Nose-First. Towards an Olfactory Gaze for Digital Art History', forthcoming.

underground in a temperature-controlled environment in bottles that are sealed from the air by argon gas.[72] Just as in the paper archive, the inevitable decay of archived scents can be slowed but not stopped. The disciplinary divisions that have created the materially dry, textual and visual bent of the humanities have been mirrored in the archives we use. But this is not the case for other disciplines. Where archives of scent have existed, their intended use and the terms on which they are accessed have differed from the collections that the humanities have traditionally drawn on. Smell's uneasy relationship with archival and historical practice has not stopped it from being taken seriously in the art world or the commercial flavour industry. Of the olfactory archives that have appeared over the course of the twentieth century, the majority are private, artistic or commercial chemical enterprises: for example, the groundbreaking archive of scent curated by the artist Sissel Toolas or the compendium of scents kept by International Fragrance and Flavors Inc.[73] Scents have seeped through the cracks of the archival systems on which humanities scholars rely. But they have collected and accumulated in other archives.

However, in the last few years great strides have also been made in the process of archiving smell for historical and heritage purposes. Both scholars and creatives have also developed forms of 'recording' that mirror the processes of phonography and photography (and require similar care and caveats in their use and interpretation). Scent-traps coated in polymer resin can capture contemporary heritage scents, the volatile organic compounds present in them can be identified in the laboratory, and a chemical blueprint can be devised for archival storage and later reproduction.[74] The archival storage of smells does not need to be in a volatile format but can be in the form of chemical recipes. Historical scents can also be produced as part of a longer process of recreation and remediation. An eighteenth-century pot-pourri recipe, followed to the

---

[72] For discussions of the Osmothèque, see Cecilia Bembibre, 'Archiving the Intangible: Preserving Smells, Historic Perfumes, and Other Ways of Approaching the Scented Past', in Adeline Grand-Clément and Charlotte Ribeyrol (eds.), The Smells and Senses of Antiquity in the Modern Imagination (London: Bloomsbury, 2022), pp. 155–173; Dugan, *The Ephemeral History of Perfume*, pp. 187–8.

[73] For some examples, see Cecilia Bembibre, 'Archiving the Intangible'; for the IFF, see their 'Fragrance Ingredients Compendium', https://www.iff.com/portfolio/products/fragrance-ingredients/online-compendium [accessed 23/02/2021].

[74] Anna Chen, 'Perfume and Vinegar: Olfactory Knowledge, Remembrance, and Recordkeeping', *The American Archivist*, 79:1 (2016), pp. 103–20; Bembibre and Strlič, 'Smell of Heritage', pp. 1–11.

letter using historical methods, can then be re-analysed by contemporary noses and chemical techniques – from paper recipe, to experimental practice, to attentive analysis by nose and machine.[75] Some historians have turned their noses up at forms of sensory recreation and re-enactment, arguing that they tell us more about contemporary preoccupations than past practices of sensing.[76] Yet turning a print recipe into a recreated perfume or using extracted VOCs to recreate and preserve historical smells does not seem especially different from converting an eighteenth-century book into a digitized edition via OCR and double-keyed text or the conversion of a late-nineteenth-century wax cylinder recording to an MP3. All of these are material manipulations, or 'transductions', of which historians must be aware, that produce new archival objects. These are forms of archiving that are also, as all such acts are, a form of re-mediation that creates new records in the process.[77]

To this a humanist might reply: what about smelling itself? The suggestion has been that whilst we can archive smells it is far more difficult to archive embodied perception. The subjectivity of smell means that any archive of smell would be a personal and private one.[78] Yet most scholars of the past would recognize that there are 'vast intellectual and practical ways in which our most private inner life, our most potent experiences, are always already parsed, structured and interpreted in ways that we do not choose'.[79] Whilst Kant might have argued that the experience of smell was fleeting and momentary, this ignores the conscious and unconscious structures, skills and habit-forming processes that lead up to and extend beyond any momentary sniff.[80] We can attempt to distil and document these habits and the meanings

---

[75] C. Bembibre, S. Barratt, L. Vera and M. Strlič. 'Smelling the Past: A Case Study for Identification, Analysis and Archival of Historic Potpourri as a Heritage Smell', in J. Bridgland (ed.), *ICOM-CC 18th Triennial Conference Preprints, Copenhagen, 4–8 September 2017*, art. 1601 (Paris: International Council of Museums, 2017).
[76] Mark Smith, 'Producing Sense, Consuming Sense, Making Sense: Perils and Prospects for Sensory History', *Journal of Social History*, 40:4 (2007), p. 841.
[77] On digitization and remediation see Adam Hammond, *Literature in the Digital Age* (Cambridge: Cambridge University Press, 2016), pp. 57–81; on sound technology and transducers see Sterne, *The Audible Past*, p. 284.
[78] Uri Almagor, 'Odors and Private Language: Observations on the Phenomenology of Scent', *Human Studies*, 13:3 (1990), pp. 253–74.
[79] C. J. Millard, 'Using Personal Experience in the Academic Medical Humanities: A Genealogy', *Social Theory and Health*, 18 (2020), p. 195.
[80] On habit and smell see Tullett, *Smell in Eighteenth-century England*, p. 13; Bruce Curtis, 'I Can Tell by the Way You Smell: Dietetics, Smell, Social Theory', *Senses and Society*, 3:1 (2008), pp. 5–22.

that they produce in language, creating an archive of perception to mirror our archive of odorants. In doing this the idea that the body itself can be an archive – especially common in cultures which do not share western European traditions of archival knowledge – needs to be taken seriously.[81] Community history and crowd-sourcing have offered useful ways of recording olfactory perceptions for posterity.[82] The evolution of ethnographies that incorporate sensory heritage, alongside forms of smell-walking and mapping, will also be central in the effort to archive odours for the future.[83] These new, explicitly olfactory, archives will begin to move us beyond the needle-in-a-hay-stack experience, in which existing meta-data makes smell so hard to find.

Sniffing around

But we can also extract smells from existing archives. Despite attempts to ventilate and control their atmospheres, libraries and archives certainly have a distinctive smell. The glue, ink and leather that go into book-making produce distinctive scents as the volumes age and they sometimes still carry the scent of their old owner's odours: tobacco, damp or perfume.[84] In her ruminations on time spent in the archive with eighteenth-century French records, Arlette Farge described the 'smell of the manuscripts' as 'trail markers' in the historians progress, whilst the archive room itself had an 'unmistakable smell, a mixture of wax and the light fragrance of faded leather bindings' that was sometimes punctuated by the 'peppery perfume' of a particular archivist.[85] The translator, historian and former director of the National Library of Argentina, Alberto

---

[81] Chen, 'Perfume and Vinegar', pp. 112–13.
[82] On smell panellists see Bembibre and Strlič, 'Smell of Heritage'; on community history see Lisa Murray, 'Big Smoke Stacks: Competing Memories of the Sounds and Smells of Industrial Heritage', in Joy Damousi and Paula Hamilton (eds.), *A Cultural History of Sound, Memory and the Senses* (London: Routledge, 2017), pp. 179–93; on crowd sourcing, see the D-Noses 'Odour Observatory' maps and Its 'Odour Collect' app: https://dnoses.communitymaps.org.uk/welcome and https://odourcollect.eu [accessed 24/02/2021].
[83] For the former, see fantastic work of Alex Rhys-Taylor, *Food and Multiculture: A Sensory Ethnography of East London* (London: Bloomsbury, 2017); for the latter, the ground-breaking practice of Kate McLean, including https://sensorymaps.com/?projects=two-centuries-of-stink-widnes [accessed 01/03/2021].
[84] David McKitterick, *The Invention of Rare Books: Private Interest and Public Memory, 1600–1840* (Cambridge: Cambridge University, 2019), p. 69.
[85] Arlette Farge, *The Allure of the Archives*, trans. Thomas Scott-Railton (New Haven, CT: Yale University Press, 2013), pp. 52, 118.

Manguel, asserted that for the library to promote imagination 'I must allow my other senses to awaken … to smell the wood of the shelves, the musky perfume of the leather bindings, the acrid scent of my yellowing pocket books'.[86] For historians today the archive itself is in a constant state of going off, as conservationists battle against decay. The advent of digitization has caused a renewed attention to the sensory traces of the archive that resist computerization.[87] But the post-paper archive is no different. From the late 1930s to the late 1980s microfilm was printed on a cellulose acetate base, the chemical decay of which produces the smell of 'vinegar syndrome', which can also infect the films around it.[88] Of course computers have also produced their own characteristic odours, especially the slightly older units that can be found in many under-funded archives.[89] At this point you might like to smell.

Olfactory Figure 2.1 *This book and any other number of books you have around you (try, if you can, to sniff of varying vintages and materials).*

As any historian will recognize, the average archive, museum or library is full of smells. However, the odorous volatility of historical objects is more than just an element in the feverish experience of archival atmospherics. The distinctive smell of old books is produced by the slow decay of their paper pages. The volatile organic compounds which produce the unique smell can be examined by heritage scientists in order to discern the level of degradation.[90] These methods do not just apply to paper. Work on the preservation of polymers in archives – ranging from plastic objects to celluloid film – has deployed techniques of gas chromatography mass spectrometry to analyse the volatile organic compounds given off by objects and thereby ascertain their rates of decomposition.[91] Machine noses can detect and deconstruct the odorous compounds that fly about our archives. They are a reminder that the archive

---

[86] Albert Manguel, *The Library at Night* (London: Yale University Press, 2008), p. 17.
[87] Emily Robinson, 'Touching the Void: Affective History and the Impossible', *Rethinking History*, 14 (2010), pp. 503–20; Jenny Newell, 'Old Objects, New Media: Historical Collections, Digitization and Affect', *Journal of Material Culture*, 17:3 (2012), pp. 287–306.
[88] Nicholson Baker, *Double Fold: Libraries and the Assault on Paper* (London: Vintage, 2002), p. 41.
[89] Jaakko Suominen, Antti Silvast and Tuomas Harviainen, 'Smelling Machine History: Olfactory Experiences of Information Technology', *Technology and Culture*, 59:2 (2018), pp. 313–37.
[90] Matija Strlič et al., 'Material Degradomics: On the Smell of Old Books', *Analytical Chemistry*, 81:20 (2009), pp. 8617–22.
[91] Katherine Curran et al., 'Classifying Degraded Modern Polymeric Museum Artefacts by Their Smell', *Angewandte Chemie International Edition*, 57:25 (2018), pp. 7336–40.

and our surroundings are in a continual process – however slow or often unnoticeable – of material fluidity, decay and change.

When we turn to distant or non-human forms of smelling, we can also find an archive of odours in the world around us. Take, for example, industrial waste. As gas-lighting began to spread in the 1810s and 1820s, gas companies had to develop ways of treating coal gas that removed some of its more toxic ingredients: odourless carbon monoxide, the rotten-egg stink of hydrogen sulphide, and the urinous smell of ammonia. The process, using slaked lime and water, produced a substance that came to be known as 'blue billy'. This material, named for its colour and similarity to Prussian blue, could not be reused and emitted a rancid, unusual, stench. The substance was therefore buried. Removing smells from coal gas above ground meant attempting to bury more odours below ground. The smell of buried blue billy – the bitter almond scent of cyanide – emerged from the rivers, sewers and ground that it polluted. As reports from the first half of the nineteenth century testify, its inhalation could cause suffocation and death. Blue billy's odours not only threatened the health of early-nineteenth-century townsfolk: they are still a threat today. The Fakenham Gas Works was opened in 1846 and is the only complete extant town gasworks in England. In 2001, a heap of blue billy was removed from the site after it was decided that it was threat to the health of the public who visited the works and its museum.

There are novel ways of seeking out such materials. For example, Natalie Jeremijenko and her students fitted VOC detectors to robot toy dogs and let them loose in areas of high historical pollution. The robo-dogs sniffed out the areas of highest contamination and huddled on them as a pack.[92] However, often the noses of local inhabitants can be equally useful. In the 1790s, a Scottish manufacturer, Charles Tennant, developed chloride of lime. The creation of this substance, which was initially used to bleach textiles but which became one of the chief deodorizers and disinfectants of choice in long-nineteenth-century Europe, actually produced large quantities of sulphurous smoke. A nineteenth-century poem by a local resident described the odours of the St Rollox chemical works in Glasgow, where chloride of lime was manufactured:

---

[92] William J. Turkel, 'Intervention: Hacking History, from Analogue to Digital and Back Again', *Rethinking History*, 15:2 (2011), p. 289.

Where fragrant zephyrs never blow,
But smutty is its atmosphere –
When rain falls dense and winds are low,
Its sulph'rous elements appear.

When winds blow south, a cloud by day
It may at once be seen and felt,
For smarting eyes then own its sway,
Through muffled noses then 'tis smelt.[93]

Around the St Rollox factory, which closed in 1964, the sulphurous products of chemical production can still be detected. The waste chemicals from the works were dumped in an area of Glasgow that now plays host to a cemetery and blocks of flats. Local residents claim that you can still smell the sulphurous stench of hydrogen sulphide coming out of the ground on a hot summer's day – the result, in part, of the soil being disturbed as new train tunnels were dug into the contaminated earth.[94]

Existing archives can also provide olfactory information to the researcher that might well be useful, if only we learn to engage with close-smelling as well as close-reading. In an oft-repeated example, Paul Duguid tells the story of a postal historian of nineteenth-century Portugal who deployed such a method. During disease outbreaks in Portugal, as in many other parts of Europe in the eighteenth and nineteenth centuries, letters were fumigated with vinegar to disinfect them. The historian sniffed the letters for the faint traces of 150-year-old vinegar and, in the process, was able to discern the temporal and geographical spread of cholera outbreaks.[95]

History as a discipline has been slow to open its other senses. This suggests that what is lacking is not an *inability* to preserve or catalogue odours but an *unwillingness* to pay attention to smelling or take it seriously. The ephemeral status of smell, in its resistance to archiving, and its supposed lack of utility in historical inquiry are a product of our low historical valuation of it.

---

[93] Hugh Aitken Dow, *History of St. Rollox School, Glasgow* (Edinburgh: Murray and Gibe, 1876), p. 177.
[94] Craig Williams, 'Remembering "Stinky Ocean" and the Smell That Forever Tortured Glasgow Noses', Glasgow Live, 16th February 2021, https://www.glasgowlive.co.uk/news/history/stinky-ocean-north-glasgow-sighthill-17755449.
[95] John Seely Brown and Paul Duguid, *The Social Life of Information* (Boston, MA: Harvard University Press, 2017), pp. 163–4.

This has also meant we have ignored more-than-human noses. In East Germany in the 1970s the secret police – the Stasi – operated their own smell archive. Here they collected – from bodies or belongings – the odours of criminals and political dissidents. These were then placed in rows of air-tight jars. Whilst humans made the archive and controlled access to it, they were not really its intended users. The scents were consulted by the Stasi's canine companions and used to track criminals and anti-communists.[96] As Eira Tansey has noted, archivists 'think of records as something created, by, for, and about humans'.[97] In an era of environmental uncertainty this assumption is being interrogated with increasing urgency. Smell is a good place from which to start our questioning. Our anthropocentric archival practice has led us to ignore the possibilities of letting other noses and ways of sensing lead the way.

But it has also been based on an under-appreciation of our own olfactory abilities. The idea that human olfaction is worse than dogs is itself a culturally constructed myth. As far back as the classical period the senses of humans and animals had been compared and that comparison has helped define the 'human'. The supposedly lower and bestial sense of smell was often said to be more sensitive in animals, especially dogs. In early modern sources ranging from allegorical images to Shakespearian drama and from philosophical treatises to hunting manuals the sagacity of the non-human nose had been emphasized.[98] As the imagined gap between animal and human was widened and solidified in the eighteenth century, the *sensitivity* of animal noses in detecting scent was contrasted with the *selectivity* of human noses in distinguishing the delightful and the disgusting.[99] By the nineteenth century sanitary inspectors attempting to sniff out traces of cholera in London slums were satirized as animal-like: in an image from 1832 several inspectors crouch on all fours and their porcine postures and bodies align with the watchful snout of a curious pig to make the connection between scent-tracking and animality.[100] However, recent

---

[96] Mark Smith, 'Transcending, Othering, Detecting: Smell, Premodernity, Modernity', *Postmedieval: A Journal of Medieval Cultural Studies*, 3:4 (2012), pp. 380–1; it should be added that this has included the present author; see Tullett, *Smell in Eighteenth-century England*, p. 13.
[97] Shannon Mattern, 'Field', in Nanna Bonde Thylstrup et al. (eds.), *Uncertain Archives: Critical Keywords for Big Data* (Cambridge, MA: MIT Press, 2021), p. 229.
[98] Steven Connor, 'The Menagerie of the Senses', *Senses and Society*, 1:1 (2006), pp. 9–26.
[99] Tullett, *Smell in Eighteenth-century England*, p. 40.
[100] 'A London Board of Health hunting after cases like cholera', 1832, chalk lithograph, 14.2x23.7cm, Wellcome Library no. 1998i.

neuroscientific studies have shown that humans can track scent, and their ability to do so improves with practice.[101] Human olfaction is not worse than that of animals. Rather, human olfaction is better at detecting some odorants than dogs whilst canine olfaction is better at detecting others.[102] Human, animal and machine forms of smelling can all alter our relationship to the archive in the future and the way we capture, preserve and access archival odours.

We have the methodologies and techniques to create and to read archives of smell. To do so we can couple the use of close smelling – including training in how to use our noses – with forms of distant smelling through the methods of analytical chemistry. The analogy with close and distant reading here is deliberate. Where distant-reading relies on computational techniques to reveal the micro- and macro-levels of text that might be obscured to the human eye, distant smelling uncovers the smells and odorants that the human nose is less able to detect or categorize.[103] When close and distant smelling is joined to close and distant reading, the words on the page take on a new light. Both can tell us something about the changing cultural fate of smells. At this point you might like to smell.

Olfactory Figure 2.2 *Root beer and some – especially in the UK – rubs and sprays for muscle pain from high street chemists.*

This is the scent of wintergreen. Studies in the 1960s and 1970s suggested that UK noses detected an unpleasant medicinal odour, whilst in the United States participants rated this as the most pleasant of all the scents they sniffed. The reasons were a combination of the chemical and the cultural: methyl salicylate was present in medicines deployed in the UK during the Second World War, whilst in the United States the same compound was more often found in sweets and root beer.[104] Both smelling and reading are historical skills and they take

---

[101] Jess Porter et al., 'Mechanisms of Scent-Tracking in Humans', *Nature Neuroscience*, 10 (2007), pp. 27–9.
[102] John P. McGann, 'Poor Human Olfaction Is a 19th-century Myth', *Science*, 356:6338 (2017), eamm7263.
[103] Hannu Salmi, *What Is Digital History?* (London: Polity, 2021), p. 34.
[104] Rachel S. Hertz, 'I Know What I Like: Understanding Odor Preferences', in Jim Drobnick (ed.), *The Smell Culture Reader* (Oxford: Berg, 2006), p. 196.

time and practise to learn. In both we are distilling our findings into, to use a term common to reading texts and analysing scent, 'notes'.[105]

By placing the contemporary smells and noses in the realm of public history and heritage – outside the boundaries of historical method – we fail to consider the experimental, performative or interdisciplinary methodologies that historians might draw on in their own research. We should be careful not to dismiss the heuristic potential of working with smells and noses. As in the museum, criticisms of sniffing in humanities research seem to stem from the interpretative bent of these disciplines. The latter has been criticized by Hans Ulrich Gumbrech, who has distinguished between meaning and presence-centred modes of enquiry, calling for humanists to give more space to the latter.[106] But most sources – from texts and material culture to images and sound – tend to be 'read' by historians. Smell is compared against this benchmark and found wanting. As we have suggested above, smell *can* be used to read documents – we just need to develop the tools and techniques to recognize odours. But smell can also tell us different things to texts in different ways. Historically, the understanding of how smelling works has been limited by a tendency to try and understand it by analogy with vision. Recent attempts to understand smell on its own terms have led to scientific and philosophical breakthroughs in how we comprehend the workings of olfaction.[107] Similarly, the heuristic potential of smell in the humanities is also ignored if we assess its utility by the standards of the visual, textual or merely interpretative.

So, beyond close and distant smelling that aligns with close and distant reading, we should ask what else smell can contribute to our historical method. I want to give some brief examples in which the use of smell can tell us something different from or beyond the understanding offered by texts. In my teaching I have often delivered sessions on early modern humoral medicine. I want my students to understand the dominance of a system in which the line between food and medicine was blurred and in which the categories hot,

---

[105] Both reading texts and analysing scents involved breaking up their components and distilling them into identifiable 'notes'. The use of 'notes' to describe the component parts of perfumes was pioneered by the Victorian perfumer Septimus Piesse; see Catherine Maxwell, *Scents and Sensibility: Perfume in Victorian Literary Culture* (Oxford: Oxford University Press, 2017), pp. 23–5.

[106] Hans Ulrich Gumbrecht, *The Production of Presence: What Meaning Cannot Convey* (Stanford: Stanford University Press, 2004).

[107] A. S. Barwich, *Smellosophy: What the Nose Tells the Mind* (London: Harvard University Press, 2020), pp. 308–10.

dry, cold and moist described the healthiness of foods instead of invisible calories and chemical constituents. I therefore get them to smell and eat food, encouraging them to try and describe the food using early modern perceptual categories. In doing so I do not hope to make my students taste like early modern subjects. Instead, I want them to get an understanding of historical distance – an understanding that will help them comprehend the radically different way early modern communities engaged with food and medicine.

A similar, more controlled, experiment has been performed by Nils-Otto Ahnfelt and his team at Uppsala University. They deployed smell panels – often used in the perfume and odour regulation industries – to sniff the scents of seven early modern medicines and then describe them. You might like to try this yourself by smelling.

Olfactory Figure 2.3 *Saffron threads – the sort you might find in a supermarket.*

Here the primary component you are sniffing is safranal, a molecule found in rooibos tea and lemons and which is now sometimes used in modern perfumery as part of a leather chord. Whilst saffron was used for culinary purposes in the early modern period, it also served a wide range of medical functions. Saffron was an expensive material and its smell was both a valued property and a way of indicating its quality.[108] Ahnfelt and his team showed that many elements of early modern sensory description have subsequently been lost, since the objects which the contemporary panel compared the odours to either did not exist (plastics, to which myrrh was compared), were materially different (shoe polish, to which saffron was compared) or would have been rare (petroleum, again this is a comparison made for saffron) in the early modern period. These insights allow us to reflect on the subsequent historical changes that have contributed to the development of different languages of smelling.[109]

We can also deploy our noses – and the noses of others – in our understanding of material culture. For an example here we can turn to Sarah Newstead and Tânia Manuel Casimiro's work on Portuguese earthenware vessels known as

---

[108] Johann Ferdinand Hertodt, *Crocologia: A Detailed Study of Saffron, the King of Plants*, trans. Sally Francis and Maria Teresa Ramandi (Leiden: Brill, 2020).
[109] Nils-Otto Ahnfelt, Hjalmar Fors and Karin Wendin, 'Historical Continuity or Different Sensory Worlds? What We Can Learn about the Sensory Characteristics of Early Modern Pharmaceuticals by Taking Them to a Trained Sensory Panel', *Berichte zur Wissenschafts-Geschichte*, 43:3 (2020), pp. 412–29.

púcaros, which released (and continue to release) a distinctive smell when filled with water. This was a property that seventeenth-century consumers valued – and they say as such in the written sources – but southern European people still find the scent evocative of homes, grandparents and childhood in the twenty-first century.[110]

Finally, if the history of smell needs to be more inter- and multi-sensory, then recreating the scents of the past can help us better grasp the interaction between their olfactory and other sensory qualities.[111] One of the most interesting examples of this in practice comes from James McHugh's work on medieval South Asian religion. It was not until remaking the perfumed pastes used in rituals that McHugh realized the importance of their bright colours. When recreated and placed in the spaces where these rituals took place, it was clear that a sensory hierarchy was at work in which some worshippers could smell the perfumes, and some could only see them in the form of the brightly coloured pastes.[112]

These three examples demonstrate the various possibilities smelling offers in informing our research and teaching practice. In using our noses, we need not give in to simplistic ideas about our ability to really smell the past. To the contrary, smell helps us better comprehend the complex dance of difference and similarity, distance and intimacy, that characterizes our contemporary engagement with the past. As these examples show, the use of our nose can often reveal both the continuities and marked differences between the perceptions of people in the past – as recorded in texts – and the particular cultural and social functions of smells today. If smelling can help us understand something about the use of material objects in the past, it can also contribute to an appreciation of the ongoing cultural heritage value of the same objects today. Finally, using our senses as part of our research practice can help us get beyond the merely symbolic or representational in order to consider the impact of the sheer material presence of 'stuff' in the past.

---

[110] Sarah Newstead and Tânia Manuel Casimiro, 'What's That Smell? New Directions for Materials Studies', *Antiquity*, 94:377 (2020), p. 4.

[111] For claims that sensory history should be more multi- and inter-sensorial, see Mark Smith, *Sensing the Past: Seeing, Hearing, Smelling, Tasting, and Touching in History* (Berkeley, CA: University of California Press, 2007), pp. 126–7.

[112] James McHugh, 'Seeing Scents: Methodological Reflections on the Intersensory Perception of Aromatics in South Asian Religions', *History of Religions*, 51:2 (2011), pp. 156–77.

3

Narratives

In the first chapter, I argued that humanities scholars should use their noses to better understand their subject position and sensitize themselves to implicit olfactory presences in the remnants of the past. In the second chapter, I made the case that both archives of smell and the smells of archive can be interpreted through new, interdisciplinary, methods that are attentive to human, more-than-human, and machine noses. I now want to turn to the stories we tell *about* smell and argue that we are better able to tell those stories *with* and *through* smell. If we are to take seriously the contention that we can extract history from scents, that 'scent is steeped in history' and 'filled with stories, with narrative images', then we can also think about how we can in turn re-fill scent with those stories in order to communicate them to audiences.[1] To understand how we can tell stories about the past using smell we have to first turn to the types of temporalities smelling instantiates.

Olfactory Figure 3.1 As you read this chapter, you could, if you so choose, burn a stick of incense.

Incense clocks found in China and Japan up until the end of the nineteenth century told time through the burning of a trail of incense. When European missionaries first encountered these time-telling techniques, they were dismissive. Matteo Ricci wrote from early-seventeenth-century Beijing:

---

[1] Byung-Chul Han, *Scent of Time: A Philosophical Essay on the Art of Lingering,* trans. Daniel Steuer (London: Polity, 2017), p. 45.

> As for their clocks, there are some which use water, and others [which use] the fire of certain perfumed fibres made all of the same size; besides this they make others with wheels which are moved by hand – but all of them are very imperfect.[2]

Europeans took this view, which separated the use of time-telling from the religious and scholarly contexts in which it was often deployed in seventeenth-century China, because scent suggests a different relationship to time to that with which Europeans were becoming increasingly familiar. The passing of the hours is filled with scents that blur into each other as the trail burns through one blend and into the next.

In contrast to the empty time of the ticking watch's hands, which leaves silent acoustic space in-between, the scent of the incense clock fills the time that it marks with a sense of duration. For the Ongee, a group that live on the Little Andaman Island in the Bay of Bengal, smell is central to time. Birth, growth and death are expressed by scents or their absence, whilst day and night are distinguished by body's emission and absorption of odours.[3] In England, well into the twentieth century, the smells of weekly rituals of washing and baking or the seasonal rhythms of harvest, haymaking and newly turned earth were integral to experience of time.[4] When the early-twentieth-century poet Edward Thomas penned an exploration of thinking 'only with scents', he focused on the smells of seasonal cultivation in the countryside.[5] In all of these examples, in quite different ways, smell fills time and is full of time.

Thus far in the humanities, our studies of smell in the past have tended to knit odour into existing periodizations, chronologies and narrative emplotments. Stories of modernization and deodorization, of urbanization and re-odorization, or of disenchantment and the disempowerment of the nose have dominated discussion of smell's pasts. When we start our investigation of past scents from the perspective of smell's historical and contemporary relationship

---

[2] Silvio A. Bedini, 'The Scent of Time. A Study of the Use of Fire and Incense for Time Measurement in Oriental Countries', *Transactions of the American Philosophical Society*, 53:5 (1963), p. 22.
[3] Constance Classen, 'McLuhan in the Rainforest: The Sensory Worlds of Oral Cultures', in David Howes (ed.), *Empire of the Senses: The Sensual Culture Reader* (London: Routledge, 2005), pp. 153–6.
[4] Douglas J. Porteous, 'Smellscape', *Progress in Physical Geography*, 9:3 (1985), p. 367.
[5] Edward Thomas, 'Digging', quoted in Andrew Motion, *The Poetry of Edward Thomas* (London: Random House, 1980), p. 163.

to temporality, some very different ways of structuring our accounts emerge. Scent acts in a nested way, like a series of tables that fit within each other, containing multiple meanings, stories and temporalities.[6]

The scent of time

Influenced by the legacy of Marcel Proust and his madeleine, we often think about the temporality of smell in terms of memory. In this framing, scent has an ability to bring the past into the present. A long tradition of writing stretching back into the early modern period has noted the particular power of smell in conjuring memories of past people, places, objects and events.[7] In the eighteenth century, writers had already recognized that the 'violent confrontation of the past and present engendered by recognition of an odour' could allow the individual to situate themselves within time: it made the self 'feel its own history and disclose it to itself'.[8]

However, this is only one example of the relationship between smell and temporality. Smell has also tended to signal a general sense of age or of old-ness. From ancient thinkers such as Plato to the present smell has been seen as the product of change in bodies and therefore an index of positive or problematic ageing –from patina to putridity. Mould and decay emit a 'sickly smell that one can almost fancy to be the smell of time'.[9] Using the nose to detect the freshness of food or the distinction between the smell of new and old books offers two examples of smell's use in discriminating age.[10] Historically this has led some thinkers to argue that 'we can smell only what is in the process of wasting away'.[11]

---

[6] Clare Brant, 'Scenting a Subject: Odour Poetics and the Politics of Space', *Ethnos*, 73:4 (2008), pp. 544–63.
[7] Catherine Maxwell, *Scents and Sensibility: Perfume in Victorian Literary Culture* (Oxford: Oxford University Press, 2017), pp. 66–7.
[8] Alain Corbin, *The Foul and the Fragrant: Odor and the French Social Imagination* (London: Harvard University Press, 1986), p. 82.
[9] Alexandre Dumas, *The Count of Monte-Cristo* (London: Routledge, 1858), p. 437.
[10] On smell and the freshness of food see William Tullett, *Smell in Eighteenth-Century England: A Social Sense* (Oxford: Oxford University Press, 2019), pp. 43–7.
[11] G. W. F. Hegel, *Aesthetics. Lectures on Fine Art,* trans. Thomas Malcolm Knox, 2 vols. (Oxford: Clarendon Press, 1998), I, 138.

As we have already seen, in travel writing and descriptions of urban geographies this general association between smell and age has often been drawn upon to mark people, places or cultures as uncivilized, regressive and Other. Consider, for example, a classic statement of 'atmo-orientalism' from a late-nineteenth-century writer describing Melbourne's Chinese quarter, in which the area is conjured as a strange, vague and threatening cloud that erupts from a historically distant world:

> I defy him to forget the peculiar smell which will there and then regale his olfactories. Even Shakespeare could not imagine anything in that line going beyond 'a most ancient and fishlike smell'; but the odour I am speaking of beats this by many degrees. De Quincey would have described it as immemorially old, distinctly Asiatic, heterogenous, and unspeakable.[12]

If this extract signals the work of smell in creating a sense of 'past-ness', it also suggests the way in which habit and culture create frameworks for the future interpretation of smells. The odour of fish is the central thread in a long history of othering, abjection and discrimination. From the fishlike smell attached to Caliban by Trinculo in Shakespeare's *Tempest*, to nineteenth-century atmo-orientalist descriptions of Chinese diasporic communities, and all the way to the present in which sufferers from trimethylaminuria (which causes the sweat to smell like fish) continue to face stigma and exclusion.[13] As this suggests, the experience of smelling does not just bring the past into the present. Smelling is also anticipatory, with past olfactory experiences and meanings setting up future ones.

The act of smelling is best described as uniting past, present and future together. Taking the idea of smelling-as-performance literally again, we can turn to theatre for an example. On the early-seventeenth-century English stage foul-smelling squibs, containing sulphurous brimstone and saltpeter, were used to create flashes and bangs. In certain theatrical contexts this scent had time-bending implications. In Shakespeare's *Macbeth* the stink of squibs linked the eschatological time of Satan and hell, medieval mystery drama, the

---

[12] D. Blair, 'The Memory of Smells', *Notes and Queries*, 4th Series, VII, 18th May (1871), p. 413; on atmo-orientalism see Hsuan Hsu, *The Smell of Risk*.

[13] Nat Lazakis, *Body Odor and Biopolitics: Characterizing Smell in Neoliberal America* (New York: McFarland, 2021).

politics of the Gunpowder Plot and the lost scent of incense to which sulphur had been opposed in a pre-reformation olfactory world. Bringing their memories and habits to the theatre, the audience would have experienced the stench of the squib a vertiginous collapsing of temporalities. Smell then offers 'a polychronicity: that is, a palimpsesting of diverse moments in time, as a result of which past and present collide with each other'.[14]

The polychronicity of smell is one reason why mapping offers a particularly interesting way of understanding the impact of odours. Consider, for example, the 'Two Centuries of Stink' project in which a map was produced that portrayed the shifting smellscapes of Widnes, in the north-west of England. Since the nineteenth century Widnes had been home to a number of offensive manufacturing plants, especially those associated with alkali production. The town's reputation was international: in 1881 an American writer noted that 'Widnes is a town of evil odour, with chemical works, soap factories, bone-manure works, and copper-smelting houses'.[15] The further widening of the ontological gulf between offense to the nose and danger to health in the nineteenth century meant that chemists, sanitarians and medical statisticians were able to argue that the odours of Widnes were not deleterious and that the habituation of the population to the smell dealt with the only issue – the offensiveness of the odours.[16] The town has continued to battle with foul smells throughout its history, including pollution from sludge incinerators and animal rendering. The 'Two Centuries' project's map, based on archival sources and contemporary noses, compressed the odours of two centuries into a layered cartography of concentric ambiences that overlap and interweave. At points the lines build up on top of each other, creating a density of colour that suggests the thickening and accretion of Widnes' olfactory atmospheres over time.[17] The map evokes the way in which the atmosphere itself is a palimpsest in which odours appear, disappear and reappear through long historical processes of writing, rewriting and overwriting the air.

---

[14] Jonathan Gil Harris, 'The Smell of Macbeth', *Shakespeare Quarterly,* 58:4 (2007), p. 467.
[15] Elisee Reclus, *The Earth and Its Inhabitants, Europe: VI The British Isles* (New York: D. Appleton and Company, 1881), p. 271.
[16] Watson Smith, 'Manufacture of Alkalis and Acids', *Transactions of the Sanitary Institute,* XIV (1894), pp. 178–80; 'Noxious Vapours and Health', *English Mechanic and World of Science,* 28:704 (1878), p. 28.
[17] Kate McLean, 'Two Centuries of Stink: Widnes', https://sensorymaps.com/?projects=two-centuries-of-stink-widnes [accessed 16/02/2022].

The material culture of smell has also emphasized its polysynchronicity. For example, the early modern period saw plague outbreaks across Europe. In response individuals, households and authorities attempted to fight the dangerous smells that were thought to cause disease with aromatic prophylactics and purifiers. One mobile prophylactic against scent was the pomander: balls of perfumed paste or containers filled with aromatic ingredients that were worn on a chain at the neck, wrist or waist. These could be sniffed as required but were also thought to create an aromatic boundary around the individual that warded off dangerous atmospheres.[18] Pomanders acted against future airs, protecting against possible danger in the atmospheres of cities, but their smells were also thought to act in the present by managing the passions of the wearer. The ingredients in pomanders included materials such as civet and musk which were widely known for their long-lasting properties. This led to their being used as fixative in perfume – molecules that added longevity to perfumes by decreasing their volatility. These odours – apt to cling to objects long after the person had departed – produced their own trails and left their own material archives in which past presence could be detected by scent. In his 1583 pamphlet The Anatomy of Abuses, Phillip Stubbes, the famously sniffy cultural critic, attacked the pride associated with

> fragrant Pomanders, odorous perfumes, and such like, whereof the smell may be felt and perceiued, not onely all ouer the house, or place where they be present, but also a stones cast off almost, yea, the bed wherein they haue laid their delicate bodies, the places where they haue sate, the clothes & things which they haue touched shall smell a week, a moneth and more after they be gone.[19]

Pomanders created their own environmental archive.[20] The carriers themselves were also designed to evoke both time's passing and future danger. One common design for pomanders was the shape of the skull and they therefore

---

[18] Tullett, *Smell in Eighteenth-century England*, pp. 160–73; Holly Dugan, *The Ephemeral History of Perfume: Scent and Sense in Early Modern England* (Baltimore: Johns Hopkins University Press, 2011), pp. 110–16; Evelyn Welch, 'Scented Buttons and Perfumed Gloves: Smelling Things in Renaissance Italy', in Bella Mirabella (ed.), *Ornamentalism: The Art of Renaissance Accessories* (Ann Arbor: University of Michigan Press, 2011), pp. 13–39.
[19] Phillip Stubbes, *The Anatomie of Abuses* (London: Richard Jones, 1583), p. 51.
[20] Elizabeth D. Harvey, 'Affect, Perfume, and Early Modern Sensory Boundaries', *Resilience: A Journal of the Environmental Humanities*, 5:3 (2018), pp. 31–50.

acted as a kind of memento-mori that encouraged their users to reflect on the passing of time and the future – and current – presence of death.[21] Given the pomander's complex temporality, it is unsurprising that the first portable watch – or at least the earliest portable watch that we know to still exist – was in the form of a pomander. Produced in 1505 in Nuremberg, the watch borrowed the shape and chain-attachment from the pomander and, no doubt, its complex interweaving of past, present and future.

The pomander-watch is a curious artefact because it sits at the boundary of two different senses of time. Scent, as represented by the pomander, produces a polysynchronous moment of presence that is full of time – past, present and future. The watch on the other hand represents – or rather would eventually represent from the early modern period onwards – an empty, continuous, compartmentalized, linear and reliably measurable time. On the one hand, we have a multi-temporal, multi-layered and heterogeneous notion of time. On the other hand, we have a time that is relentlessly propelled onwards – tick, tick, tick.[22]

The temporality of scent-less-ness

To a large extent that second time, the time of the watch, is also a component in the time that many humanities scholars – especially historians – engage with. This is the modern historicist notion of time that flows irreversibly forwards and that in turn emphasizes the unbridgeable gap that separates the past from the present. Many of the most influential narratives in the study of past smells fit into the linear, historicist, conception of time. The deodorization narrative – in which the eighteenth century inaugurated a long sanitary march to the clean and pleasant land of modernity – and the anosmia narrative – in which the sense of smell has lost importance and our noses have lost their sensitivity over time – both depend on this linear ordering.[23]

---

[21] Holly Dugan, 'Seeing Smell', in Jackie Watson et al. (eds.), *The Senses in Early Modern England, 1558–1660* (Manchester: Manchester University Press, 2015), p. 103.

[22] On the shifting notions of time, see Stuart Sherman, *Telling Time: Clocks, Diaries, and English Diurnal Form* (Chicago: University of Chicago Press, 1996); Paul Glennie and Nigel Thrift, *Shaping the Day: A History of Timekeeping in England Wales 1300–1800* (Oxford: Oxford University Press, 2009).

[23] These two narratives are summarized in Mark Jenner, 'Follow Your Nose? Smell, Smelling, and Their Histories', *American Historical Review*, 116:2 (2011), pp. 335–51.

These are modernization narratives; they emphasize progress, and in doing so they nestle within a series of other -izations, including urbanization, industrialization and secularization.

Most work by historians interested in smell – including this author's previous publications – deploys a fairly linear, historicist, plotting. This is because scholars are often less interested in smells *per se* and more interested in the social, cultural or epistemological fate of smelling. For example, scholars have been interested in the impact of the European reformations on the relationship between scent and the sacred or the role of late-nineteenth-century bacteriology in transforming the link between smell and disease.[24] In other cases, historians have mined key historical transformations for their odours from urbanization and colonization to wars and revolutions.[25] What collectively emerges from this scholarship is a kind of olfactory seismograph, in which scholars are detecting and plotting the odours or altered olfactory perceptions produced by key historical events or processes.

Whilst a critique of the historicist understanding of time had existed in various forms throughout much of the twentieth century, it is only in the last twenty years or so that scholars interested in the past have begun to take it seriously.[26] Historians have turned to tracing the multiple temporalities that have existed in past societies. To take a few examples: the late medieval world was home to a multitude of overlapping temporalities created by music, calendars, religious observance and work habits; early modern Europeans did not share the preoccupations with time-telling 'accuracy' that have preoccupied modern historians of time; and the idea of multi-temporality and the resistance to a

---

[24] Jacob M. Baum, 'From Incense to Idolatry: The Reformation of Olfaction in Late Medieval German Ritual', *The Sixteenth Century Journal*, 44:2 (2013), pp. 323–44; David S. Barnes, *The Great Stink of Paris and the Nineteenth-century Struggle against Filth and Germs* (Baltimore: Johns Hopkins University Press, 2018).

[25] Alexander M. Martin, 'Sewage and the City: Filth, Smell, and Representations of Urban Life in Moscow, 1770–1880', *Russian Review*, 67:2 (2008), pp. 243–74; Meg Parsons and Karen Fisher, 'Historical Smellscapes in Aotearoa New Zealand: Intersections between Colonial Knowledges of Smell, Race, and Wetlands', *Journal of Historical Geography*, 74 (2021), pp. 28–43; Nicholas J. Saunders et al. (eds.), *Modern Conflict and the Senses* (London: Routledge, 2017); Jan Plamper, 'Sounds of February, Smells of October: The Russian Revolution as Sensory Experience', *American Historical Review*, 126:1 (2021), pp. 140–55.

[26] For an overview, see Marek Tamm and Laurent Olivier, 'Introduction: Rethinking Historical Time', in Marek Tamm and Laurent Olivier (eds.), *Rethinking Historical Time* (London: Bloomsbury, 2019), pp. 1–22.

historicist notion of time developed out of the crisis of the First World War.[27] These accounts increasingly discuss time through metaphors of percolation, sedimentation, and the spiral or folded pleat rather than the line.

These understandings of temporality seem especially useful for understanding smell. For an example, we can turn to the decidedly linear deodorization narrative in which it is argued that techniques of ventilation, lavation and disinfection have – since the eighteenth century – rendered 'our' worlds less and less odorous. One criticism of such a narrative is that it positions those living today at the *end* of a historical process of deodorization that is ostensibly accepted as a contemporary norm. Whilst it might be easy for academics sitting in air-conditioned and regularly cleaned offices to emphasize 'our own deodorized modern life and the richly scented lives of our forebears', it is unclear whether those who live next to waste dumps or paper mills, with multiple chemical sensitivities, or the more-than-human actors with which we co-exist – from dogs and cats to birds and bees – would agree.[28] By accepting that we live in a deodorized world today, some works charting the evolution of modern deodorized bodies and environments are also perpetuating the stigmatization of those who are deemed odorous and therefore not 'normal'.[29]

Responding to the deodorizing narrative – and its associations with 'modernity' – scholars interested in the medieval and early modern periods have consistently argued that there is nothing new about a fear of bad smells or attempts to get rid of them.[30] In fact, nineteenth- and twentieth-century modernity produced more smells than it removed – from the waste produced by massive urbanization to the odorous outputs of automobiles, manufacturing

---

[27] Matthew S. Champion, *The Fullness of Time: Temporalities of the Fifteenth Century* (Chicago: Chicago University Press, 2017); Stefan Hanß, 'The Fetish of Accuracy: Perspectives on Early Modern Time(s)', *Past and Present*, 243:1 (2019), 267–84; Lucian Hölscher, 'Mysteries of Historical Order: Ruptures, Simultaneity, and the Relationship of the Past, Present, and Future', in Chris Lorenz and Berber Bevernage (eds.), *Breaking up Time: Negotiating the Borders between Past, Present and Future* (Göttingen: Vandenhoeck and Ruprehct, 2013), pp. 134–53.

[28] David Howes, Constance Classen and Anthony Synnott, *Aroma: The Cultural History of Smell* (London: Routledge, 1994), p. 13.

[29] This is an argument made persuasively by Nat Lazakis, *Body Odor and Biopolitics: Characterizing Smell in Neoliberal America* (Jefferson: McFarland, 2021), pp. 37–61; Michelle Ferranti, 'An Odor of Racism: Vaginal Deodorants in African-American Beauty Culture and Advertising', *Advertising & Society Review* (2011), doi: 10.1353/asr.2011.0003.

[30] Carole Rawcliffe, *Urban Bodies: Communal Health in Late Medieval English Towns and Cities* (Woodbridge: Boydell, 2013); Dolly Jørgensen, 'The Medieval Sense of Smell, Stench, and Sanitation', in Ulrike Krampl et al. (eds.), *Les cinq sens de la ville du Moyen âge à nos jours* (Tours: Presses Universitaires Francois-Rabelais, 2013), pp. 301–13.

and industrialized slaughter on the battlefield. One response to these apparent continuities has been to turn to universalist, biologically determinist, ideas about an innate human tendency to avoid certain bad smells.[31] Another has been to emphasize that the link between smell, disease and deodorization is an example of a set of ideas and practices that submerge and re-emerge throughout history at different points in time in different communities.[32] To resolve this tension between continuity and change, I suggest that we need to attend the polysynchronic nature of smell and the temporalities through which deodorization works.

When used to describe the material state of social life and environments, 'deodorized' is a misnomer. Every deodorization is really a re-odorization and 'another olfactory encoding'.[33] Take, for example, the history of tobacco and social space: when pipe-smoking was deemed impolite in some late-eighteenth-century coffee houses, it meant that the scent of sweaty feet and bad breath assailed the noses of patrons instead.[34] When smoking bans have been introduced in the twenty-first century pub-visitors have been left with the odour of 'years of spilt beer and flatulence', the 'acidic odour of the chemicals used in the loos' and the smells of crowded bodies.[35] Getting rid of some odours, or moving them to other spaces, means altering olfactory geographies rather than rendering them inert or absent.

Deodorization is best understood not as a material state but as a technique of power that is used to create and reify boundaries between inodorous selves and odorous others based on race, class, gender, religion and other forms of identity. Seen from this perspective, the success of deodorization is always dependent on it being unsuccessful, incomplete and provisional. It always implies a series of pasts, presents and futures – as it defines itself against a supposedly odorous past while looking to an ever-moving horizon of inodorousness. For example, in an 1860 article in the popular publication – *The English Woman's Journal* – a

---

[31] Leona J. Skelton, *Sanitation in Urban Britain, 1560–1700* (London: Routledge, 2016), p. 36.
[32] William Tullett, 'Re-Odorization, Disease, and Emotion in Mid-nineteenth-century England', *The Historical Journal*, 62:2 (2019), pp. 765–88.
[33] Mark Jenner, 'Civilization and Deodorization? Smell in Early Modern English Culture', in Peter Burke et al. (eds.), *Civil Histories* (Oxford: Oxford University Press, 2000), p. 144.
[34] Tullett, *Smell in Eighteenth-century England*, pp. 149, 151.
[35] Ruaridh Nicoll, 'Strike a Light, Smokeless Pubs Stink', *The Guardian*, 31st October 2004, https://www.theguardian.com/uk/2004/oct/31/smoking.comment [accessed 11/02/2022].

writer under the name 'A Haunted Man' described a series of memories evoked by smell: from the gas lighting in early-nineteenth-century theatres to the smell of old books found in a childhood rummage through an old attic. One scent that haunted the writer was chloride of lime. At this point you might like to sniff (carefully, without breathing too much in).

Olfactory Figure 3.2 *Bleaching powder or liquid bleach (the active ingredient of which is chloride of lime). Just a quick sniff ...*

From the 1790s onwards, when chloride of lime was first developed as a bleaching agent in textile manufacture, it became the smell of institutions, states and bureaucracies at work: from the atmospheres of schools in the 1830s, to sanitarians in the 1840s attempting to deodorize cesspits and sewage, through homes, hospitals and workhouses in the 1860s, and into the battlefields of the First World War where chloride of lime used to deodorize toilets, disinfect dead bodies and render water safe (but not pleasant) to drink.[36]

The 'Haunted-Man' identified that the issue with chloride of lime – as with the rosemary used in the seventeenth century against the plague or the carbolic soap used in the later nineteenth century in germicidal hygiene – was that it left its own scent. These smells, rather than suggesting safety, quickly became associated with the very thing they attempted to cover up or remove:

> Many and many a time have I smelt chloride of lime, and yet never without feeling for an instant that sudden sinking of the heart, that indescribable stony dread and terror which accompanied my first experience of an infectious fever in the house.[37]

The memory of the smell of chloride of lime became predictive of dangerous infection, causing individuals to anticipate the presence of atmospheric danger and therefore to act accordingly. To put it another way, 'by proposing itself as the counteragent of shit, perfume only ensures its persistence; denial only

---

[36] Theodore Dwight, *The School-master's Friend, with Committee-man's Guide* (New York: R. Lockwood, 1835), p. 260; Tullett, 'Re-Odorization, Disease, and Emotion in Mid-nineteenth-century England', pp. 765–88; Ernest Abraham Hart, *An Account of the Condition of the Infirmaries of London Workhouses* (London: Chapman Hall, 1866), p. 13; Steve Hurst, 'The Senses: Battlefield Exploration, Drawing and Sculpture', in Nicholas J. Saunders and Paul Cornish (eds.), *Modern Conflict and the Senses* (London: Routledge, 2017), p. 353.

[37] A. Haunted Man, 'Every-day Ghosts', *The English Woman's Journal*, 5:30 (1860), pp. 37–40.

makes the proof more positive – shit is there'.[38] Attempts to cover, repress or avoid smells only serve to ensure the perpetuation of the affective atmospheres associated with them. In the same way, the pasts of smell also continually re-emerge and resurface in the present and serve to predict, anticipate or determine olfactory futures.

The nineteenth-century's outpouring of futurological fiction illustrates deodorization's temporalities at work. In the future city the atmosphere would be 'pure and sweet', the odours of slums would disappear, ozone-producing instruments would regulate the air, energy would be produced without odour and atmospheric regulation would govern the use of scents.[39] Yet they also illustrate how this deodorization has always been deferred. Several authors predicted that in the future home the odours of the kitchen would be removed without disrupting the rest of the building. This was hardly a new concern – it was an architectural problem that had been wrestled with since antiquity.[40] This concern had not gone away because, despite architectural change, new forms of ventilation, and the supposedly deodorizing impulses of Western medicine, sanitation and culture, the rise of the iron stove and waste-water plumbing in the second half of the nineteenth century had actually re-odorized spaces and created a greater number of potential stenches.[41]

Another example comes from cremation which, by the late nineteenth century, several individuals in Britain and America were promoting as a way of dealing with the offensive odours and unsanitary diseases that came with burying dead bodies.[42] Yet cremation released its own odours: governments suggested they

---

[38] Dominique Laporte, *History of Shit*, trans. Nadia Benabid and Rodolphe El-khoury (Cambridge: MIT Press, 2002), p. 87.

[39] 'London a Hundred Years Hence', *The Leisure Hour*, 6 (1857), pp. 701–3; Bradford Peck, *The World A Department Store: A Story of Life under a Cooperative System* (Boston, 1900), pp. 26–7; Russell T. Baron, *A Hundred Years Hence: The Expectations of an Optimist* (London: T. Fisher Unwin, 1905), pp. 25–6; Herbert Gubbins, *The Elixir of Life: Or, 2905 A.D.; a Novel of the far Future* (London: H. J. Drane, 1914), pp. 94–5; Robert Grimshaw, *Fifty Years Hence, or, What May Be in 1943* (New York: Practical Publishing Co., 1892), pp. 51, 67.

[40] For ancient kitchens and smells see Hannah Platts, *Multisensory Living in Ancient Rome: Power and Space in Roman Houses* (London: Bloomsbury, 2019), pp. 193–230; for an eighteenth-century example, see Sean Takats, *The Expert Cook in Enlightenment France* (Baltimore: Johns Hopkins University Press, 2011), pp. 46–7.

[41] On gas stoves see Melanie Kiechle, *Smell Detectives: An Olfactory History of Nineteenth-century Urban America* (Seattle: Washington University Press, 2017), pp. 97–8; on waste-water plumbing see J. Lane Notter and R. H. Firther, *The Theory and Practice of Hygiene* (London: J. & A. Churchill, 1896), pp. 497–8.

[42] F. Julius Le Moyne, *Cremation. An Argument* (Pittsburgh: E.W. Lightner, 1878), pp. 9–10; Sir H. Thompson, *Modern Cremation: Its History and Practice* (London: Paul, Trench, Trübner, 1891), pp. 76, 82, 88.

should only be used where they did not produce foul odours, families had to stay away from cremators so that they were not disturbed by the smells they emitted, and inventors attempted to engineer out the olfactory evidence of burning bodies.[43] In 1903, William Stanley produced a utopia set in 1950 where cremation had become the norm – but even then the smells of burning bodies could be detected, wafting out from the islands to which crematoriums had been relocated.[44] In Anthony Trollope's 1882 satirical dystopia, *The Fixed Period*, compulsory euthanasia at the age of sixty-eight is followed by cremation. But workers refuse to run the furnaces because of the smells of the bodies and the crematoria have to be moved so that the smell does not scare the population.[45] In the end, smell is a spectral presence, always waiting in the wings, its banishment never quite successful and always pushed further into the future.

By locating deodorization in a future that was yet to come, these texts served to remind readers just how far they had to go. In Edward Bellamy's hugely popular novel *Looking Backward 2000–1887*, the travelling narrator returns to Boston in 1887, having visited the socialist utopia of the year 2000. His first impressions are olfactory:

> A dozen times between my door and Washington Street I had to stop and pull myself together, such power had been in that vision of the Boston of the future to make the real Boston strange. The squalor and malodorousness of the town struck me, from the moment I stood upon the street, as facts I had never before observed.[46]

In Bellamy's 1897 work, *Equality* – a sequel to *Looking Back* – an olfactory relic of the past is preserved in order to present a lesson in the dangers of inequality. In the new city with its wide airy boulevards Bellamy's narrator discovers an unusual ruin:

> I found myself face to face with a typical nineteenth-century tenement house of the worst sort … reeking reservoirs of foetid odors, kept in by lofty, light-excluding walls …. It seemed to exhale an atmosphere of gloom and chill which all the bright sunshine of the breezy September afternoon was unable to dominate.[47]

---

[43] Douglas J. Davies and Lewis H. Mates (ed.), *Encyclopedia of Cremation* (Farnham: Ashgate, 2005).
[44] William Stanley, *The Case of the Fox: Being His Prophecies, under Hypnotism, of the Period Ending A.D. 1950: A Political Utopia* (London: Truslove & Hanson, 1903), p. 164.
[45] Anthony Trollope, *The Fixed Period* (London: William Blackwood and Sons, 1882).
[46] Edward Bellamy, *Looking Backwards from 2000 to 1887* (Boston: Ticknor & Co., 1888).
[47] Edward Bellamy, *Equality* (London: William Heinemann Limited, 1897), pp. 62–3.

The narrator's chaperone Edith informs him that these are 'ghost buildings' and a sign outside the house adds that 'this habitation of cruelty is preserved as a momento to coming generations of the rule of the rich'.[48] A deodorized future cannot exist because deodorization as a technique requires the continued presence of smell in order to have any kind of meaning.

The Victorian 'Haunted Man' that we encountered earlier described smells as 'every-day-ghosts'. The idea that smells are in some way haunting is a powerful one that resonates with smell – and deodorization's – polysynchronous temporalities. Deodorization can accurately be described as 'hauntological': 'the ghostly folding of space and time where the present, past and future cannot be cleanly divided but rather are co-constitutive, with each always containing traces of each other'.[49] This spectral presence is sometimes also described as awareness of lost futures, of futures we have been taught to anticipate, which never materialize, but which not infrequently re-appear mirage-like in the near distance. Rather than understanding it as a programme of change that happened in the nineteenth and twentieth centuries, deodorization can more accurately be described as a lost future – an impossible goal that is always receding from view and that haunts not just our presents but our futures. Deodorization, like the stench of explosive squibs on the seventeenth-century stage, is best understood as a polysynchronous encoding of smell.

The archaeology of an odour

As a re-appraisal of deodorization's temporalities demonstrates, thinking of smell's pasts in linear temporal terms obscures as much as it reveals. An alternative to narratives that trace lost smells, smell loss or shifting attitudes to smelling has been to focus on case studies of smells with particular significance in a period or place. Examples of this approach include studies of early modern ambergris, eighteenth-century sulphur and the modern olfactory history of

---

[48] Ibid., p. 63.
[49] Michael Buser, 'The Time Is out of Joint: Atmosphere and Hauntology at Bodiam Castle', *Emotion, Space and Society*, 25 (2017), p. 9.

the durian fruit.⁵⁰ Starting from the assumption that people have used – and continue to use – their noses in different ways depending on place, time and practice, these studies have been inspired by the call for 'a history of smells, exploring the cultural meanings of particular odours in specific locations or within particular discourses, rather than a history of smell'.⁵¹ Thus far this type of work has involved a careful attention to textual references to smell and the mapping of its meanings across different genres and communities. Smell becomes the meeting point of multiple histories: for example the scent of garlic leads us into histories of cuisine, class, medicine, national identity and racism.⁵² In these histories, smell operates as a narrative trip-wire that, when knocked, causes our histories to shoot off in a multitude of potential directions. The scent of a process, object or material is the thing being held materially or semiotically constant, whilst researchers trace the shifting perceptions of those scents over time.

This is especially clear in the few examples where smell has been used as a prompt for oral history. Oral historians have increasingly included questions about sensory experience in their interview schedules. When asked about smell interviewees are often able to reflect on the odours of particular places from their past. In a study of the Sydney neighbourhood of Balmain interviewees recalled the smell of the chemical, sugar and soap factories that defined the smellscape of the area in the 1960s.⁵³ Remembering life in Alexandria, New South Wales during the 1950s some recalled the 'industrial smell' whilst others recalled the sickly sweet smell of jam-making or the 'beautiful' smell of a factory producing tomato sauce.⁵⁴ Interviewees in a study of Poland's post-communist transition noted that Soviet-era Poland was characterized by the smells of cooking and

---

[50] Sophie Read, 'Ambergris and Early Modern Languages of Scent', *The Seventeenth Century*, 28:2 (2013), pp. 221–37; Emily Friedman, *Reading Smell in Eighteenth-century Fiction* (Lewisburg: Bucknell University Press, 2016), pp. 99–118; Andrea Montanari, 'The Stinky King: Western Attitudes toward the Durian in Colonial Southeast Asia', *Food, Culture and Society*, 20:3 (2017), pp. 395–414.
[51] Mark Jenner, *'Civilization and Deodorization?'* (Oxford: Oxford University Press), p. 138.
[52] Ibid.
[53] Paul Hamilton, 'The Proust Effect: Oral History and the Senses', in Donald A. Ritchie (ed.), *The Oxford Handbook of Oral History* (Oxford: Oxford University Press, 2012), pp. 219–32.
[54] Lisa Murray, '"Big Smoke Stacks": Competing Memories of the Sounds and Smells of Industrial Heritage', in Joy Damousi and Paula Hamilton (eds.), *A Cultural History of Sound, Memory, and the Senses* (London: Routledge, 2016), p. 183.

disinfectant associated with communal housing whilst the post-1989 era saw an increased sensitivity to the distinction between perfumed middle classes and ostensibly less hygienic working classes.[55] Interviewees seem quite able to discuss the smells of their past when asked.

However, a small number of examples have illustrated the power of smells themselves – rather than questions *about* smell – in stimulating recollection. Taking a more smell-first approach, these studies have used smells as prompts for oral history narratives and as tools that enable participants to explore the memories associated with them. In the 'Snidge Scrumpin' study conducted in Wolverhampton – in an area of the UK known as the Black Country – participants responded to scents that included lemon, paint, herbal sweets and canal water. These smells evoked memories from participants' pasts in a series of temporal and geographical ripples: 'starting with a memory contained to an intimate, safe family space ... the memory starts to spread outwards, coming to absorb more and more places, public buildings, paths – until the entire town is evoked'.[56]

There are two points that this emerging scholarship helps us to make. Both are important in making the case that we can construct arguments about the past in olfactory form.

The first is that the pasts evoked by smells in the present are not just spontaneous but involve exploration and thought by those doing the sniffing. The cumulative impact of work in psychology, neurosciences, philosophy, literature, sociology and anthropology has been to suggest that the sense of smell is useful in detecting, discriminating, learning and communicating; that it can be cultivated for aesthetic interrogation and thoughtful reflection; that it can evoke both involuntary or voluntary memories; and that the human sense of smell is both an affective and an intellectual tool.[57] Smell can therefore provide a medium for constructing meaningful stories and arguments about

---

[55] Martyna Śliwa and Kathleen Riach, 'Making Scents of Transition: Smellscapes and the Everyday in "Old" and "New" Urban Poland', *Urban Studies*, 49:1 (2012), pp. 23–41; Christoph Neidhart, *Russia's Carnival: The Smells, Sights, and Sounds of Transition* (New York: Rowman and Littlefield, 2002).

[56] Sebastian Groes and Tom Mercer, 'Smell and Memory in the Black Country: The Snidge Scrumpin' Experiments', in Sebastian Groes and R. M. Francis (eds.), *Smell, Memory, and Literature in the Black Country* (Basingstoke: Palgrave Macmillan, 2021), pp. 59–80.

[57] See the first eight chapters of Larry Shiner, *Art Scents: Exploring the Aesthetics of Smell and the Olfactory Arts* (Oxford: Oxford University Press, 2020), summarized at pp. 138–40.

the past. It is perfectly plausible that our noses can be trained to deconstruct, understand and critique stories narrated in scent. We can build up a knowledge of the presences and meanings that smells would have accrued at a moment in time and index that knowledge against odorous molecules in the present.

The second point to make is that the smells used in the 'Snidge Scrumpin' study will not have precisely matched the total smellscapes in which similar scents may have been sensed by participants and they may not have in fact been a complete match for the original objects that the scents were designed to evoke. For example, the smellscape of a home would no doubt have included other scents beyond those of cooking faggots and the precise composition of 'canal water' may have differed slightly in the past and present. Nonetheless, these scents were able to stimulate memories and evoke pasts connected to scents. There is a good reason for this. Whilst a scent is made up of hundreds of molecules, humans can often only detect a minority of them, and there are certain molecules in any one scent contributing to the distinctive smell that human noses associate with it – the 'lemon-ness' of a lemon smell or the 'paint-ness' of a paint smell can be evoked through particular molecules.

One criticism of deploying smells in contemporary reconstructions is that the odours we deploy today will be materially different to the odours of the past.[58] This is certainly true when we think about perfumery: a bottle of civetone or synthetic civet oil today is a very different proposition to the brown, waxy, secretion produced by civet cats in the early modern period and used to perfume gloves. Nonetheless there are certain key molecules that give natural civet its scent and that can be combined in a synthetic civet oil: civetone, muscone, indole and skatole. These collected molecules allow civet to float between the musky, sweet, animal and faecal – a categorization that is as familiar to us today as the seventeenth- and eighteenth-century satirists who found comic potential in civet's excremental perfume.[59] The excretions of a seventeenth-century civet cat and the synthetic civet oil produced in a twenty-first-century laboratory might be materially different, but it seems reasonable to argue that they may share many of the molecules that produce the civet-y scent.

[58] Dugan, *The Ephemeral History of Perfume*, p. 10.
[59] Tullett, *Smell in Eighteenth-century England*, p. 29.

As I have already suggested, work that has traced the histories of particular smells has often implicitly assumed a degree of material continuity around which meanings coalesce and change. What if we think about this material constancy in terms of collections of molecules that make up smells? A 'smell studies' field that takes the molecular materiality of smells seriously in its engagement with the past, present and future will be closer to archaeology than history in the temporalities that it evokes and traces.

To understand what I am suggesting here we have to be clear about what is meant when we talk about 'smells'. In English, 'to smell' is both transitive and intransitive – it refers both to the emission of odours and their perception. 'Smell' can be properly described for our purposes as the meeting point of the cultural and the chemical, the moment where our learnt habits and perceptions meet with the compounds that make up odours. A history of 'smells' is thus a history of the point at which noses meet molecules and in doing so evoke a polysychronous mixing of pasts, presents and futures. These smells are akin to an archaeological event which

> simultaneously influences past, present and future. It becomes part of a pre-existing memory, which it alters. It creates a new situation in the present, and its presence is destined to influence the creations that will follow.[60]

If we take the understanding of odours as a palimpsest seriously then we should usefully see them as archaeological objects. An archaeological method involves tracing the accretions of pasts in the material world that surrounds us today. We can equally say that we are interested in tracing the memories, meanings, times and places that have been deposited and embedded in odorous molecules over time. To think in this way requires us to move from thinking about odours as things that jog our memories to odours as things that are invested with time and memories or as containers into which we pour 'smell' (those moments of meeting between noses and odorous molecules).

'Sulphurous' or 'sulphur' is a good example here. Sulphur as an element is inodorous and yet the term 'sulphurous' is an oft-used olfactory descriptor.

---

[60] Laurent Olivier, 'The Business of Archaeology Is the Present', in Alfredo Gonzalez-Ruibal (ed.), *Reclaiming Archaeology: Beyond the Tropes of Modernity* (London: Routledge, 2013), p. 128.

The molecule often associated with 'sulphurous' is hydrogen sulphide, which has a smell which is variously described as a rotten eggs, rotten vegetables or rotten cabbage. Over time, the scent has acquired associations with a whole range of processes, materials and places, a series of meanings that have become layered and sedimented, but which frequently resurface. Sulphur's rich history includes associations with the devil, hell and the supernatural; medicinal and scientific links with spa waters, Paracelsian medicine and volcanic geologies; and industrial processes and outputs ranging from the production of coal gas to vulcanized rubber. These meanings – all linked to hydrogen sulphide – might often be evoked together. For example, Charles Frederick Cliffe, visiting the Lower Swansea Valley in Wales in 1854, described how the

> the copper smoke is a serious nuisance to the country around, injurious both to cattle and herbage … At night the Swansea Valley forms no bad representation of the infernal regions, for the smell aids the eye. Large groups of chimneys and ricketty flues emit sulphurous arsenical smoke.[61]

When two scents appear similar to us, as in the case of sulphurous smells, it is partly because those scents may share particular molecules that give them similar olfactory properties. This means that smells often 'suggest or echo or rhyme with different things in the world'.[62] Tracing those olfactory echoes is one way of engaging with the palimpsestic qualities of smell. The temporal and spatial qualities of smell make it a potent tool for creating stories that emphasize the blurring of past, present and future. Where typical linear conceptions of historical time tend to insist on the past as, *in* the past, separated from the present, smell can enfold temporality and geography in on itself, re-arranging periods and places into intimate interpenetration, or turn time into a spiral across which meaning and experience can skip. Using scent can, for example, bring odours back to the nose that have been redistributed across the globe through historical processes of offshoring and displacement.

If we nose our world from this archaeological standpoint, then past smells – past moments when noses have met molecules – lie latent in the scents around us. Smell is a 'fossil image, or a kind of image that contains

---

[61] John Barr, *The Assault on Our Senses* (London: Methuen, 1970), p. 106.
[62] Harold McGee, *Nose Dive: A Field Guide to the World's Smells* (London: John Murray, 2020).

the material traces of the past within it'.[63] By taking molecules that made up the odours of the past – and continue to make up odours in the present – and learning to re-connect particular osmologies and meanings with them today we are learning to retrieve the pasts or times embedded or collected in odours. This process of reconnection or reconstruction, of learning to articulate the meanings, practices and presences that are or have been associated with particular groupings of molecules, is a process of gathering the smell of odours – that polysynchronous meeting of noses and molecules – together and understanding their relationship to each other. This includes not just the pasts and presents of odours but also their anticipatory futures.

Beyond see-what-you-smell

So far, this chapter has suggested that smells are best understood through forms of polysynchronicity rather than linear historicist narratives; that olfactory practices such as deodorization often imply multiple temporalities; and that, if we think about the study of smell as a process of archaeology, we can excavate and re-assemble the multiple smells (understood as multi-temporal moments when noses meet molecules) of odours in the present. In the final section, I want to pursue what it might mean – indeed what it might smell like – if we were to attempt to publish the results of such work in a format that was designed to be smelled. This does not mean attempting to put together an interpretation of 'how the past smelled'. Instead, it involves using odour as a medium for staging smells that can then be understood and engaged with. At one level this is no different to our tendency to offer up interpretations of the past in words. We do not tend to assume that a text outlining an academic interpretation of the past is attempting to get the reader to experience 'how the past read' to those in the period under discussion. We accept that what is being provided is an interpretation, narration or staging of the past using tools, techniques and disciplinary conventions.

But offering an argument or narrative through smell is doing something more than this, since it involves both a tool for both the 'presentification' and

---

[63] Laura U. Marks, *Touch: Sensuous Theory and Multisensory Media* (Minneapolis: University of Minnesota Press, 2002), p. 114.

'articulation' of the past. The presentation of historical arguments in olfactory form – with accompanying textual explanation of the particular processes, spaces and meanings associated with an olfactory argument's component smells – is a form of presentification in that it involves the

> ... *literal* transhistorical (yet not ahistorical) transference or relay of metonymic and material fragments or traces of the past through time to the 'here and now' – where and when these can be activated and thus realized once again in our practical, operative, and sensual engagement with them.[64]

In this context, odorous molecules are metonymic material fragments of past smells that are re-activated by our sensorial re-engagement with them. But this process of presentification is also a process by which the past is articulated. By articulation, I mean that we are able to register differences and similarities, changes and continuities, between past olfactory cultures and our own. For example, you might like to sniff.

Olfactory Figure 3.3 *Dried or fresh rosemary, rubbing it between your fingers to help release the scent.*

You might like to consider, briefly, the various associations you have with that scent and the various places in which you might find it today. You might also consider the other scents that it echoes, rhymes with or suggests. Today many readers will no doubt be most familiar with rosemary's use in cooking meat, roasting vegetables or as part of herbal teas. Plenty of seventeenth- and eighteenth-century recipes also record culinary uses for rosemary.[65] You might detect the herb's scent in the world of perfumery, since rosemary was the main ingredient in one of the earliest alcohol-based perfumes in Europe – 'Hungary water', ostensibly developed in the fourteenth century – and continues to be a note deployed by perfumers today.[66]

However, many of these earlier recipes were part of an understanding of food in which diet was deeply enmeshed humoral health, in which smell could

---

[64] Vivia Sobchack, 'Afterward: Media Archaeology and Re-presencing the Past', in Erkki Huhtamo and Jussi Parikka (eds.), *Media Archaeology: Approaches, Applications, and Implications* (Berkeley: University of California Press, 2011), p. 324.
[65] For examples see Robert May, *The Accomplisht Cook* (London: R. Wood, 1665), p. 405; Eliza Smith, *The Compleat Housewife* (London: R. Ware, 1750), p. 70.
[66] R. S. Cristani, *Perfumery and Kindred Arts* (London: Sampson Low, Marston, Searle and Rivington, 1877), p. 29.

play an important role. As you sniff, you might want to consider that the scent of rosemary was, in the seventeenth century, considered to be 'hot' and 'dry' in humoral terms and that this explained its curative properties for headaches and migraines that were supposedly caused by an overly cold or moist brain.[67] Throughout the eighteenth and nineteenth centuries, 'Hungary Water' was not just a perfume but a remedy, gesturing to a world where the boundaries between medicinal and luxury cultures of scent were rather less blurred.[68]

The reader may be less aware of the links between the scent of rosemary and weddings or funerals where it was used in the seventeenth century.[69] They may also be less aware of its use in the same period as a preservative against plague, with rosemary used as both a prophylactic and, when burnt, as a way of disinfecting interiors. In this context, the smell of rosemary could be associated with comforting protection from disease or an anxious reminder of its lurking presence.[70] On sniffing you might have been put in mind of other, closely related odours, such as pine and camphor. This similarity, which comes from the shared pinene and camphor molecules found in these substances, is also linked to a long medical history in which the scents of camphor and pine were celebrated for their curative properties.[71] There is a medicinal quality to the rhymes and echoes of rosemary.

By sniffing rosemary today we are better able to articulate its olfactory pasts, bringing them into relation with each other and with the broad olfactory present. To paraphrase Bruno Latour's discussion of the notion of the 'subject', there is 'nothing especially interesting, deep, profound, worthwhile' in the sensory past 'by itself' and it

> only becomes interesting, deep, profound, worthwhile when it resonates with others, is effected, moved, put into motion by new entities whose differences are registered in new and unexpected ways.[72]

---

[67] George Hartman, *The Family Physitian* (London: Richard Wellington, 1696), pp. 289–90.
[68] Ambrose Cooper, *The Complete Distiller* (London: P. Vaillant, 1757), p. 153.
[69] Philip Williams, 'The Rosemary Theme in Romeo and Juliet', *Modern Language Notes*, 68:6 (1953), p. 402.
[70] Dugan, *The Ephemeral History of Perfume*, pp. 98–104.
[71] R. A. Donkin, *Dragon's Brain Perfume: An Historical Geography of Camphor* (Leiden: Brill, 1999); Clare Hickman, 'Pine Fresh: The Cultural and Medical Context of Pine Scent in Relation to Health – from the Forest to the Home', *Medical Humanities*, 48:1 (2022), pp. 104–13.
[72] Bruno Latour, 'How to Talk about the Body? The Normative Dimension of Science Studies', *Body & Society*, 10:2–3 (2004), p. 210.

The history of theatrical uses of smell offers some telling examples of this in practice. In 1891 a theatrical adaption of *The Song of Songs* was staged by Paul-Napoléon Roinard at Le Théâtre d'Art in Paris. Nine perfumes were diffused at stages in the performance, with all distributed via spray bottles except the burnt frankincense, and accompanied by particular musical themes and colours.[73] The scents were meant to evoke spirituality and poetic symbolism, but they were also popular in commercial perfumes and daily hygiene products, and the disjuncture between the two prompted humour rather than serious aesthetic appreciation.[74]

In September 1902, Sadakichi Hartmann pursued an abortive attempt at staging a 'Perfume Concert' that would use scent to take the audience on a journey to Japan. This received similarly barbed comments from critics. One problem – among many – that Hartmann faced was that his audiences had very different associations with the scents he chose. He noted that whilst for him cedarwood evoked the 'mouldering smell' of long-uninhabited houses, for audience members it variously evoked 'a shipment of Oriental goods' or 'a pencil factory in Long Island'.[75]

In Walter Reade's 1959 *AromaRama* and Hans Laube's 1960 *Smell-o-Vision* scents were pumped into cinemas at different stages of movies, in order to correspond with what could be seen on screen. Once again, the echoes produced by scent proved troubling. The scent chosen to evoke 'a beautiful old pine grove in Peking' smelled more like 'a subway restroom on disinfectant day'.[76] In the nineteenth century pine-forests had been celebrated for their health-giving odours, which led to the use of pine oil and disinfectant in hospitals, and this then led to synthetic-pine-scented disinfectants in the home including brands – such as 'Toilet Duck' – which still retain their pine-scent today.[77]

---

[73] Kirsten Shepherd-Barr, '"Mise en Scent": The Theatre d'Art's *Cantique des cantiques* and the Use of Smell as a Theatrical Device', *Theatre Research International*, 24:2 (1999), pp. 152–9.
[74] Érika Wicky, 'Perfumed Performances: The Reception of Olfactory Theatrical Devices from Fin-de-siecle to the Present Day', in Nele Wyants (ed.), *Media Archaeology and Intermedial Performance: Deep Time of the Theatre* (Cham: Palgrave Macmillan, 2019), p. 133.
[75] Christina Bradstreet, '*A Trip to Japan in Sixteen Minutes*: Sadakichi Hartmann's Perfume Concert and the Aesthetics of Scent', in Patrizia di Bello and Gabriel Koureas (ed.), *Art, History and the Senses* (Farnham: Ashgate, 2010), pp. 51–66.
[76] 'A Sock in the Nose', *Time*, 21st December 1959, p. 57.
[77] Hickman, 'Pine Fresh', pp. 104–13.

My point in offering up these examples is to argue that it is precisely the relationship between what the scents were intended to evoke and what they actually evoked that is interesting. Using our noses engages us in a process of articulating our own olfactory worlds – our osmologies – in relation to others in the past and present. It is that bringing into relation that should interest us as scholars.

Making an historical argument in or through odours also means articulating odours in relation to each other in time. In order to achieve this, we have to consider smell on its own terms rather than treating it as we would another medium. The importance of thinking through smell's own properties as a form for storytelling is also demonstrated by historical attempts to use smell to tell stories. Nineteenth- and early-twentieth-century experiments with smell and storytelling had clearly been influenced by other media, especially photography and moving images. In the 1891 staging of *The Song of Songs*, reviewers were not overwhelmingly positive about the experience and they suggested that the accumulated odours produced an unhealthy experience of olfactory overstimulation.[78] Some – though not all – reviewers of twentieth-century experiments with smell in the cinema were also critical. A review of *AromaRama* in the *New York Times* suggested that the multiple scents 'confuse the atmosphere' and that the 'purifying treatment' used to clear the air between 'suffusions of odours' left a 'sickly sweet smell, which tends to become upsetting'.[79] Another reviewer in *Time* noted that 'the smells are not always removed as rapidly as the scene requires: at one point the audience distinctly smells grass in the middle of the Gobi Desert'.[80] *Smell-o-Vision* received a slightly more favourable review in *Variety* because the film had 'mastered the quick change' and was 'able to get the smell of coffee out of the place before the load of fresh bread appears on the screen'.[81]

One of the chief problems in all of these cases was the lack of distance between perfumes, which accumulated in the performance spaces over time and mixed. This was not the intention of producers. Inspired by visual representation – the photograph and later cinema – the intended use of scent

---

[78] Wicky, 'Perfumed Performances', p. 137.
[79] Bosley Crowther, 'Smells of China; "Behind Great Wall" Uses AromaRama', *The New York Times*, 10th December 1959.
[80] 'A Sock in the Nose', p. 57.
[81] Avery Gilbert, *What the Nose Knows: The Science of Scent in Everyday Life* (New York: Crown, 2008), p. 180.

had revolved around understanding each smell as a separate, distinct, image that would follow consecutively one after the other. In reviews, the success of each theatrical or cinematic use of smell was determined by how far smell could be made to operate like, or in concert with, visual media. As so often in its history, smell was being measured in terms of how far it could do the work of vision and inevitably failing. In trying to create a historical argument in olfactory form we therefore have to be careful in thinking about how we harness smell's volatility and its patterns of geographical and temporal dispersion rather than seeing either as an obstacle.

This means trying to evoke smells both individually and collectively. In a telling quote one of the supporters of the 1959 *AromaRama* performance observed that perhaps it 'belonged in the laboratories' rather than being 'presented to a paying public'.[82] They were right in the sense that a cinema was not a laboratory and the capacity to control the dispersion of smells was simply not the same. In the 1891 performance of *Song of Songs* the scents could easily have been confused with the perfumes worn by audience members and Hartmann's 1902 performance had to deal with a boozy music-hall venue full of tobacco smoke and other competing odours.[83] Since they wanted to offer individual smells in succession, these examples of olfactory theatre experienced the blurring and blending as smells as a problem rather than a useful quality that might be harnessed to artistic ends.

However, theatrical performances were not alone in trying to separate off individual odours like this. In the seventeenth and eighteenth centuries most attempts to classify and study smells had been in natural history, botany and medicine. In this context, the study of smell had been strongly intersensorial and involved attention to both the other sensory properties of particular materials and the embodied experience of medicines. However, in the course of the nineteenth century the predominant locus for the scientific study of smell became experimental psychology. By the late nineteenth century, most attempts to study smell involved working with single odours divorced from wider smellscapes and sensory contexts. The goal was not just to get at pure smells but also at pure olfactory sensations unmediated by other stimuli.

---

[82] Ibid., p. 178.
[83] Bradstreet, '*A Trip to Japan*', p. 52.

For example, in the 1890s the Dutch psychologist Henrik Zwaademaker developed a tool for measuring the strength of odours and olfactory sensitivity known as the olfactometer. The idea here was to deliver individual smells straight to the nose through tube and the illustrations of Zwaademaker's instrument are telling in their evocation of a disembodied, floating, head with its nose applied to one end of the instrument.[84] In a description of her work published in 1898 the psychologist Eleanor Gamble records several attempts to control and isolate the odours being used and this extended to covering the walls and floor of the room in which experiments were carried out with oiled paper or oil-cloth.[85] Another solution was to separate the head from the rest of the body, which was achieved by K. Komuro in 1921 with a device known as the 'camera inodorata'. This was a box with glass and aluminium walls with a bottom cover that fitted over the neck, effectively isolating the head alone in a makeshift 'room'. Mercury vapour and ultraviolet radiation were used to get rid of any odours to obtain an 'olfactory vacuum'. Under these conditions odours were more easily detectable and, of course, could be analysed in almost complete separation from other intervening scents or sensory stimuli.[86] The camera inodorata was particularly aimed at those working in perfumery laboratories, where the proliferation of smells sometimes made work difficult. Finally, this tendency developed in ever-more-exaggerated ways in the mid-twentieth century. In 1950, psychologists at Cornell University developed an 'olfactorium', a whole room rendered 'odor-proof' via an assemblage of architectural and hygienic technologies.[87]

Despite sharing some basic infrastructure with the laboratory (such as air conditioning), trying to recreate pure olfactory encounters with individuated odours in a theatre or cinema was always going to be difficult. Theatrical impresarios and their reviewers were not the only ones to note the disjuncture between the conditions of sensory laboratories and the way people interacted with smells in the world outside them. Medics and sanitarians in the early

---

[84] Henrik Zwaardemaker, *Die Physiologie des Geruchs* (Leipzig: Wilhelm Engelmann, 1895), p. 198; Edward Wheeler Scripture, *Thinking, Feeling, Doing* (Meadville Penna: Flood and Vincent, 1895), p. 124.
[85] Eleanor Acheson McCulloch Gamble, 'The Applicability of Weber's Law to Smell', *The American Journal of Psychology*, 10:1 (1898), p. 117.
[86] D. Foster et al., 'An Olfactorium', *The American Journal of Psychology*, 10:1 (1950), pp. 431–2.
[87] Ibid., 431–40.

twentieth century were similarly disappointed. In a 1923 article in the *American Journal of Public Health*, J. R. Earp set out the difficulty of odour classification in the context of nuisance regulation. Earp suggested that the classifications of smell being developed by psychologists in laboratory experiments – in particular Earp referred to Hans Henning's 1916 smell prism with its six corners – largely dealt with odours in their 'pure' or individuated state. As Earp pointed out, this was not especially useful once one got out onto the street.[88] In 1909, a British chemist Morris J. Williams wrote to the *Lancet* to lament the lack of a vocabulary for smell – particularly when teaching the material properties of different medicines to medical students. For this purpose the author desired a series of 'pure definite chemical bodies to avoid mixed smells' and that these 'primary' smells could be used in school teaching as primary colours were. These smells would then form the basis for describing more complex scents.[89] However, respondents were sceptical for precisely the reasons outlined by Earp. The writers for *The Medical Brief*, a US journal, noted that they 'seriously doubt the working of his classification scheme in crowded districts and tenements, where it is by no means always possible to "choose pure definite bodies"'.[90]

The same concerns apply to the use of smell by humanities scholars or in heritage and museums. There are many historical examples where smells only matter in relation to each other and to zone in on single odours does little to convey the olfactory affordances of past environments. For example, the history of disinfectants and deodorizers – which often left their own distinctive odours – can only be understood in relation to the smells that they attempted to remove that included rotting bodies, stagnant water and excrement. Early modern coffee may have smelt and tasted very different, but its olfactory impact is best understood when set aside the other smells that would be found in coffee-houses, including tobacco smoke, tallow candles, perfumed wigs and freshly printed news-sheets. It is not just that coffee today, roasted and prepared according to very different methods, is different

---

[88] J. Rosslyn Earp, 'Odors: Their Sanitary Significance and Their Elimination', *American Journal of Public Health*, 13:4 (1923), pp. 284–5, 287.
[89] Morris J. Williams, 'Smells and Their Classification', *The Lancet* (1909), pp. 1795–6.
[90] *The Medical Brief*, 38 (1910), p. 222.

to its early modern equivalent: the whole sensorial context in which coffee was consumed has changed markedly.

However, there are also examples where particular modes of attention would have heightened the importance of specific, individual, scents. Consider, for example, the use of smell in the medieval Christian cult of relics. Careful sniffing could be involved in the assessment of a relic's authenticity and pilgrims could collect ampullae filled with fragrant holy water as a sensory souvenir: archaeologists suggest that a late medieval ampullae from Saint William's cult site at York Minster still contains a 'pleasant-smelling liquid' composed of aromatic and medicinal herbs and spices.[91] Certainly pilgrims would have engaged with the scents of these liquids within a wider olfactory environment, but they clearly focused particular attention on saintly scent. Alternatively, consider the rosaries made from beads of amber that would have been caressed and counted by sixteenth- and seventeenth-century Italian Catholics at prayer. The warming of the amber by touch released a distinctive scent. This smell would lie on the hands afterwards as the person went about their day and, if sniffed, give a moment of spiritual recollection that also evoked the amber burnt in churches as a form of incense.[92]

Practices of odour-making and forms of attention are crucial to how we understand and represent a smellscape. For example, recreations or scents that do not wish to evoke the total smellscape of an environment may nevertheless seek to evoke particular patterns or gestures linked to scent. Two examples from the Odeuropa project are worth considering here. The first is the smell of 'hell' developed by the Odeuropa team (in particular Sofia Ehrich, Lizzie Marx and Victoria-Anne Michel), International Flavours and Fragrance, and Museum Ulm for the 'Follow Your Nose' smell tour around Ulm's collections. The scent was to be paired with an image of Christ in Limbo by Martin Schaffner, dated to around 1549, which depicts Christ pulling Adam and Eve up through the gates of hell whilst a devil breathes fire and black smoke emerges from the infernal depths. Sermons and works of religious contemplation described

---

[91] Paul A. Brazinski and Allegra R. P. Fryxell, 'The Smell of Relics: Authenticating Saintly Bones and the Role of Scent in the Sensory Experience of Medieval Christian Veneration', *Papers from the Institute of Archaeology*, 23:1, 11 (2013), pp. 8–9.

[92] Rachel King, '"The Beads with Which We Pray Are Made from It": Devotional Ambers in Early Modern Italy', in Christine Göttler and Wietse de Boer (eds.), *Religion and the Senses in Early Modern Europe* (Leiden: Brill, 2013), pp. 167–70.

the smell of 'infernal brimstone, mixed with so many corrupted matters', a stink 'more loathsome and unsavoury than a Million of dead dogs', and the stench of the 'Putrifying exhalations of the Dead'.[93] Early modern writers noted that whilst on earth 'our fire is made for comfort ... with fuell of Wood or Cole' the fire of hell was tempered 'with all the terrible torturing ingredients of Sulphur and Brimstone ... loathsomly to perplexe the smell'.[94] The intention was to create a foul scent composed of smoky, fecal, burnt notes that matched the olfactory descriptions of hell found in early modern texts. However, we were not just interested in the smells that early moderns associated with hell, but the process by which they imagined and engaged with them. Early modern devotional manuals used by the Jesuits and several religious communities called for believers to regularly meditate on the sensory torments of hell. In these daily and weekly rhythms of prayerful focus they were asked to imagine the 'noisome stenches & pestilent smells' characteristic of sin and the punishment thereof.[95] The scent that Odeuropa created with IFF – at once beguiling and disgusting – encouraged people to sniff in a similar way, returning again and again to the odour in order to pick apart its components and consider what made it both offensive and arresting. The aim was both to combine the earthly scents early moderns associated with hell and the meditative practice in which those scents were implicated.

Another scent that Odeuropa produced as part of our collaboration with IFF, and Museum Ulm was a sixteenth-century pomander, created to accompany a 1516 portrait of Eitel Besserer, an Ulm Councillor, by the artist Martin Schaffner. The image represents Besserer in prayer, holding a wooden rosary attached to a silver filigree pomander. The portrait was a nice reminder that the pomander fulfilled multiple functions: meditative aid, luxury item and prophylactic against plague. Unlike hell, contemporary recipes for pomanders exist across Europe and provided a useful touchstone for the modern composition. However, we could not recreate the domestic atmosphere of prayer or the pungent plague-filled streets in which such a

---

[93] Jeremy Taylor, *Contemplations of the State of Man in This Life, and in That Which Is to Come* (London: H. Newman, 1698), pp. 205–6.

[94] Isaac Ambrose, *Ultima: The Last Things, in Reference to the First and Middle Things* (London: J. A., 1650), pp. 246–7.

[95] Nicky Hallett, *The Senses in Religious Communities, 1600–1800: Early Modern 'Convents of Pleasure'* (Farnham: Ashgate, 2013), pp. 57–9.

pomander might have been put to use. It could therefore be said that from an olfactory perspective we were only telling half the story.

However, the way in which the scent was delivered in the context of another Odeuropa event – our 'City Sniffers' tour of Amsterdam, composed of a rub and sniff scent card and accompanying mobile application – demonstrated that the scent could be used in a way that at least mirrored the gestural deployment of the scent and its mediating role in early modern culture.[96] Pomanders, both as balls of perfumed paste or metal containers for scented materials, were said to release their scent by tactile interaction: writers noted that a 'Pomander chafed yeelds a comfortable smell' or 'rubbing the Pomander will bring forth the sweetness'.[97] Once activated the scent might be held to the nose in order to breathe it in more deeply and to further bolster the aromatic boundary around the upper part of the body. On the Odeuropa tour of Amsterdam participants also had to rub the materials – in this case thick card onto which scent had been applied by microencapsulation – in order to release the odour and then hold it to their nose. The lingering scent on the fingers after rubbing the card also pointed to the use of pomanders and amber beads in rosaries, the scent of which would have remained on the hands after prayer. Whilst the whole olfactory experience was clearly not the same, the act of rubbing, holding to the nose, and thereby changing the relationship between the individual and their surrounding smellscape mirrored the practice of using a pomander that is found in historical sources.

We can therefore use scent to creatively plot the shifting relationship between scent and space rather than approximate the precise odours of a historical smellscape. Certain scents may also have dominated particular spaces and the dominant odours may have changed as individuals moved through them. Take, for example, the religious topography of olfaction in late medieval Antwerp. The olfactory experience of the Church of Our Lady would have altered as one moved into, through and out of the building. The competing smells of dead or diseased bodies and odours of incense would have varied as one perambulated

---

[96] For the application and an image of the card, see https://citysniffers.odeuropa.eu/ [accessed 26/08/2022] and for some context see https://odeuropa.eu/2022/08/launch-of-city-sniffers-a-smell-tour-of-amsterdams-ecohistory/ [accessed 26/08/2022].

[97] H. H., *The Workes of the Reuerend and Faithfull Servant of Jesus Christ M. Richard Greenham* (London: William Welby, 1612); Richard Baxter, *The Saints Everlasting Rest* (London: Thomas Underhil and Francis Tyton, 1650), p. 732.

the church with its many altars, crypts and statues dedicated to particular saints. The smellscape of the church would also have varied over time – the scent of incense might have filled the church more strongly in the middle of masses or the scent of the rushes used to keep the floor clean might be stronger when they had just been refreshed. Moving outside into the nearby churchyard the odour of incense might stick to the clothing and mix with other odours from the decomposing bodies and retail stalls in the Green Cemetery or the carcasses from the nearby butchers' quarter.[98] Smell fills space and is full of space as well as time. The Western European assumption that smell is *the* sense of memory does not hold fast in all cultures. In medieval South Asia smell acted not in mnemonic but in spatial terms. Smell is described in Sanskrit texts as a mediator between persons, things and spaces, causing people to move towards or away from the odour. In this context smell's mnemonic character is much less important than its spatial one.[99] The stories that we tell with scent are just as likely to be geographical, moving through worlds (or perhaps letting those worlds move through us in the form of scent), as they are temporal.

Using smell as a medium for presentification or narrativization rather than text would therefore require us to think carefully about what forms of temporality or geography are being represented and how they are being evoked. This involves attending to the discontinuous, fragmentary and episodic nature of smelling. Some smells are background, whilst others are thrust into the foreground. In original formulations of the idea of the smellscape – which drew on the earlier concept of soundscape – smell events of shorter duration were contrasted with constant smellmarks.[100] Designers distinguish between smells that are episodic, foreground and time limited with smells that are background, pervasive and constant.[101] We must also distinguish between those smells to which attention is deliberately given through interested sniffing, those that announce themselves by impinging strongly on the nose in ways that are unavoidable, and those which we might initially sniff before becoming habituated to them.

[98] Wendy Wauters, 'Smelling Disease and Death in the Antwerp Church of Our Lady, *c*. 1450–1559', *Early Modern Low Countries*, 5:1 (2021), pp. 17–39.
[99] James McHugh, *Sandalwood and Carrion: Smell in Indian Religious Culture* (Oxford: Oxford University Press, 2012), pp. 101–2.
[100] Porteous, 'Smellscape', 360.
[101] Barbara Erwine, *Creating Sensory Spaces: The Architecture of the Invisible* (London: Routledge, 2017), p. 180.

Of 'notes', 'narratives' and presences

If the humanities scholar is interested in using smell to present an argument about changing smellscapes over time or engage in the presentification of scented pasts, then they will potentially have to work with several odours at once rather than separate them and present their interrelationship in time and space. I want to suggest that perfumery and the skills of the perfumer offer a useful set of techniques and resources for putting this into practice. Perfumers are used to telling stories through smell, in ways that harness the volatility of odours, and that use layering and temporality in nuanced and complex ways. This may involve humanities researchers working with perfumers to craft arguments or it may mean scholars actively learning the skills needed to develop scents themselves. For the purposes of this short book, I want to simply suggest why there is potential in exploring this possibility.

The initial impetus for this argument came from an observed similarity between the chronotopes sometimes deployed by historians, the geographies discussed by urbanists and the basic structure often deployed in perfumery. In perfumery it is common to talk in terms of top, base and heart notes. There is a long history of thinking of perfume in terms of 'notes'. In the 1862 edition of his *Art of Perfumery*, Septimus Piesse had outlined a 'gamut' of odours that indexed the components of perfumes against musical notes, organized them along the treble and bass clefs, and discussed how perfumers might create harmonies by building bouquets of different 'chords'.[102] Whilst Piesse's gamut failed to take off, the idea of thinking of perfume in terms of 'notes' persisted. In the 1950s William Poucher and Edward Maurer helped to popularize the idea of 'top', 'middle' and 'basic' notes, with each note separated into one of the three categories by their relative volatility – the length of time it took for their distinctive scent to completely evaporate and disappear.[103] Classifying notes by volatility helped perfumers to think in terms of *time* when composing their scents. In perfumery manuals a basic structure – often represented as a pyramid – is outlined that moves from a top note which first strikes the nose

---

[102] Maxwell, *Scents and Sensibility*, pp. 23–6.
[103] W. A. Poucher, 'A Classification of Odours and Its Uses', *Journal of the Society of Cosmetic Chemists*, 6:2 (1955), pp. 81–94; Edward S. Maurer, *Perfumes and Their Production* (London: United Trade Press, 1958), pp. 60–1.

when the perfume is applied and lasts only a few minutes, through middle or heart notes which emerge after the top notes which may last anywhere up to four hours, and base notes which may last from a few hours to multiple days.[104] This suggests that if we are to seriously engage with smell as a way of making an argument this will require more than a momentary sniff. As with reading, the experience of a perfume is something that takes time. If we are to make arguments in the form of a perfume we have to learn to sit with a scent as it unfolds its multiple temporalities.

The pyramid structure, from shortest to longest duration, echoes another tripartite division of times that is often invoked in historical writing: that advocated by the *Annales* historian Fernand Braudel. In several articles in the late 1940s and 1950s Braudel outlined a conception of time that was tripartite, with each part incorporating several different facets: geographical time, social time and individual time; the longue durée structures, medium-term processes and short-term events; and different temporal speeds from the slow to the quick.[105] Braudel's temporal structure is also sometimes imagined as a triangle from short term at the top to longue durée at the broad base. Perfume should be understood, on one level, as offering a way of expressing scent over time – in a more historicist vein – or as offering us the opportunity to evoke the times contained within scent – in the more multi-temporal form advocated above. The levels of time one chooses to layer or evoke might range from centuries, decades and years to hours, minutes and seconds.

The same structure from top note through middle note to base note can also be understood as a way of mapping smellscapes and forms of olfactory attention too. Base notes are the scents that are common to a wide geographical area such as a town centre, middle or heart notes are the smells of particular streets or neighbourhoods within the wider area such as the scents of a specific factory or the smell of a fish-market, and the top notes are the scents particular to specific spaces such as the entrance to a shop.[106] The relation between these scents may change as a person moves through a space and so thinking of smell

---

[104] Nigel Groom, *New Perfume Handbook* (London: Chapman and Hall, 1992), p. 266; Robert R. Calkin and J. Stephan Jellinek, *Perfumery: Practice and Principles* (New York: Wiley, 1994), p. 88.
[105] Berber Bevernage *History, Memory and State-sponsored Violence: Time and Justice* (London: Routledge, 2011), pp. 112–16.
[106] Victorian Henshaw, *Urban Smellscapes: Understanding and Designing City Smell Environments* (London: Routledge, 2014), pp. 171–2.

in this way allows us to incorporate spatiality and temporality together. The same model can be applied to modes of attention ranging from those scents that are in the 'background', through those that impinge themselves on the nose, to those that individuals deliberately chose to attend to. What this might look like in a scent can range in terms of the levels of space it seeks to evoke from an attempt to evoke a whole neighbourhood to mapping out an individual street, through to mapping a particular building or public space.

Take, for example, the scent experienced by Pacific voyagers off the coast of New South Wales in September 1779. According to John Hawkesworth the voyagers felt

> a light breeze from the shore, which was so strongly impregnated with the fragrance of the trees, shrubs, and herbages that cover it, the smell being something like that of Gum Benjamin.[107]

If you can get hold of it then at this point then you could sniff.

Olfactory Figure 3.4 *Benzoin resin, incense or gum.*

There were multiple temporalities and geographies at work in this example, which can be pulled out by relating them to other scents. The scent was part of the temporality and geography of a sea-borne voyage that would have also involved other odours ranging from stagnant water on-board the ship, the smells of the sea air and water, and the different odours of contact when colonists made land-fall.[108] We also have the scent of biblical time being evoked here, since the fragrant smell of shorelines was linked to that of paradise before the fall, and the earthly time of Christian history that included the use of benzoin as a key ingredient in the composition of incense.[109] Here benzoin might be linked to other scents, including sulphur or the odour of sanctity. The fragrant and paradisical scent also evoked a more secular history of progress in which the

---

[107] John Hawkesworth, *Account of the Voyages*, 3 vols. (London: W. Strahan, and T. Cadell, 1773), II, 655.

[108] Alain Corbin, *The Foul and the Fragrant* (Cambridge, MA: Harvard University Press, 1986), pp. 26, 47–9, 65, 95–8, 105, 170; John Rickman, *Journal of Captain Cook's Last Voyage to the Pacific Ocean* (London: E. Newbery, 1781), p. 164; James Cook, *A Voyage Towards the South Pole*, 2 vols. (London: W. Strahan and T. Cadell, 1777), II, 385; Journal of Richard Pickersgill, Third Lieutenant of the Resolution, Captain James Cook', National Maritime Museum, London. JOD/56, 58–9.

[109] 'Trade Card of Richard Warren' (London, c.1768–1770) BM, Trade cards Banks 93.45; Sydney Parkinson, *Journal of a Voyage to the South Seas* (London: Stanfield Parkinson, 1773), p. 134.

journey across the eighteenth-century Pacific was understood – by eighteenth-century Britons – as a journey back in time. Here the fragrant land was understood in relation to the scents of mortality – body odour and excrement – and urbanizing European civilization's scents of luxury and waste.[110] Benzoin, with its vaguely vanilla-like smell, is often used as a fixative, and was a popular ingredient in seventeenth- and eighteenth-century perfumery, and so it might be evoked in relation to other ingredients in burnt perfumes, pomanders and scented waters.[111] Multiple times, multiple geographies, all evoked by putting benzoin into relation with other scents.

At this point, it is important to recognize that there is an enormous amount of scope to play with the kinds of temporality that scent can evoke. The pasts or times evoked by a scent need not evolve straightforwardly through short, medium and long term or from point A to point B. The world of perfume is one of temporal experimentation and creativity. Some perfumes shift quickly in a linear fashion from top notes to base notes whilst others take a whole day to move through their layers. But other perfumes move through a whole series of many different themes over the course of their evolution that do not necessarily follow a linear pattern. In some cases, one may feel that one is smelling a completely different scent at different stages in the perfume's lifespan. In other examples a single note persists whilst other notes come and go around it.[112] For the modern perfumer time is 'an integral part of any perfume's composition' and 'the role of the perfumer' is to 'create a succession of olfactory moments'.[113]

For a final example we can take the smell of war or more specifically the smell of war as represented by the trenches of the First World War. Clearly there are ethical and sensitivity issues with representing these kinds of smells. However, olfactory artists and museums have used difficult odours – of death or gas-warfare for example – in their engagements with historical conflicts.[114] It seems

---

[110] Johann Reinhold Forster, *Observations Made during a Voyage around the World* (London: G. Robinson, 1778), pp. 365–6.
[111] Timothy Morton, *The Poetics of Spice* (Cambridge: Cambridge University Press, 2006).
[112] Eddie Bulliqui, 'The Phenomenon of Olfactory Time', https://scentculture.institute/the-phenomenon-of-olfactory-time/#_ftnref93 [accessed 01/03/2022].
[113] Jean-Claude Ellena, *Perfume: The Alchemy of Scent*, trans. John Crisp (New York: Arcade, 2011).
[114] Stephen Miles, 'Sensorial Engagement in Tourism Experiences on the Western Front', in Nicholas J. Saunders and P. Cornish (eds.), *Modern Conflict and the Senses* (London: Routledge, 2019), pp. 81–2.

reasonable to suggest that humanities scholars can do the same, so long as warnings are given and ethical processes followed. We can take several approaches in seeking to represent the First World War trench in the form of a constructed scent. We might think about locating scents in time that represent the shifting smells of warfare over longer chronological periods or we might choose to evoke the specificity of olfactory experience in a particular context such as the trench warfare on the Western front or the field of battle at Waterloo. What follows is not a comprehensive account but aims to think about a handful of scents and how they would feature in a scent constructed to represent the diverse temporalities of that conflict.

When a ninety-six-year-old veteran attended the opening of the Imperial War Museum's trench experience in July 1990, he felt that the mix of smoke, cordite and frying bacon back took him back to his wartime experience. However, he added, 'The smell of death – that's not here.'[115] The smell of death and decay, dominated by the scents of protein and purine breakdown such as cadaverine and putrescine but shifting in its components of time, has been a recurrent part of the smellscape of war. However, the precise temporalities of this scent shifted as the nature of combat changed. For example, the smell of death dominates descriptions of the battlefield at Waterloo in 1815. However, since the battle itself was the work of a day these descriptions came from those who came to the site after the battle had finished as tourists or journalists. They note that the 'the smell from the dead horses' that lined the road from Waterloo to the battlefield itself was 'horrid' and the air of Brussels to which the wounded had been transported was 'pestilential'. Several weeks after the battle some argued that the battlefield smelled relatively 'sweet' but the one visitor, Charlotte Waldie, wrote,

> The effluvia, even beneath the open canopy of heaven, was horrible; and the pure west wind of summer, as it passed us, seemed pestiferous, so deadly was the smell that in many places pervaded the field.[116]

Walter Scott recorded similar smells of putrefaction on his visit to the battlefield in his 'The Field of Waterloo':

---

[115] Graham Heathcote, 'Museum Offers Sights, Sounds, and Smells of World War I Trench', https://apnews.com/article/9b9f2bd201ccc751e774ba98f9f18f7b [accessed 02/11/21].
[116] Cited in Paul O'Keefe, *Waterloo: The Aftermath* (London: Random House, 2014).

> And feel'st thou not the tainted steam,
> That reeks against the sultry beam,
> From yonder trenched mound?
> The pestilential fumes declare
> That Carnage has replenished there
> Her garner-house profound.[117]

Snuff and brandy were an accompaniment to some of these battlefield trips: used to dull tourist's smelling (and their other senses).

By contrast, the smell of death was a constant and ever-present one in the noses of First World War combatants. For example, see Paolo Monelli's description in 1921 of the smell of the trenches:

> Always that smell of cemetery in the nose. There are twenty of them crammed into a crevasse, which are slowly decomposing … You see the face of the medical standard-bearer change bit by bit every day, as a result of decomposition … But his eyes are always alive, and wide open … You were dead so recently, and you were already nothing, nothing more, a grey mass destined to stink huddled against the rock; … but you, man, are not and it is as if you never were. There is carbon and hydrogen sulphide under us, covered by a pile of rags-uniforms; and we call them dead. But tonight you stink too much, dead.[118]

The British soldier Private Alfred Griffin wrote that there was 'nothing like a dead body's smell. It's a putrid, decaying smell, makes you stop breathing, you think of disease. It's a smell you can't describe unless you've smelt rotten meat'.[119] A scent seeking to represent the smellscape of a battlefield would therefore be quite different depending on whether it was open Napoleonic battle like Waterloo or the grinding trench warfare most often associated with the First World War (it would be different yet again in the case of a siege, to take another example). In the case of Waterloo, the scent of death would only develop later on in the composition whilst in an interpretation of the First World War's smellscapes it would a constant note throughout.

---

[117] Walter Scott, 'The Field of Waterloo', in *The Poetical Works of Sir Walter Scott* (London: Adam and Charles Black, 1857), p. 421.
[118] Cited in Franco Nicolis, 'The Scent of Snow at Punta Linke: First World War Sites as Sense-scapes, Trentino, Italy', in Nicholas J. Saunders and P. Cornish (eds.), *Modern Conflict and the Senses* (London: Routledge, 2019), p.73fn3.
[119] Santanu Das, *Touch and Intimacy in First World War Literature* (Cambridge: Cambridge University Press, 2005), p. 84.

Another omnipresent smell on the First World War battlefield was that of chloride of lime, which we came across earlier on. Take, for example, one soldier writing to his father from Gallipoli in August 1915:

> Between the trenches are any amount of dead and decomposing bodies of our men and Turks lying on the heather. The smell is awful, though we throw down quantities of Chloride of Lime and creosote.[120]

The constant, background, presence of this scent in the trenches is communicated clearly in Siegfried Sassoon's *Memoirs of an Infantry Officer*. Attempting to lose himself in thought despite the fact that 'trench life was an existence saturated by the external senses', Sassoon is quickly brought back to those senses by the unholy crash and cloud of black smoke unleashed by a shell exploding nearby. At this point 'the trench atmosphere reasserted itself in a smell of chloride of lime'.[121]

As Sassoon's interrupted thoughts suggest, the smells of the First World War trench were regularly interrupted by the scents of fighting itself. Again, this is another example where a scent evoking the battle of Waterloo would differ from one seeking to represent the First World War. The former conflict was characterised by the scent of gunpowder weaponry including muskets, rifles, and cannon. In the late nineteenth century, the smell of gunpowder was replaced by cordite – one of a number of smokeless propellants developed from the 1860s onwards across Europe – and a burning, acrid, smell therefore replaced the sulphurous scent of gunpowder. Manuals of military chemistry, guides to explosives and official army documentation illustrate the importance of the nose in assessing propellants and their ingredients.[122] In the 1890s it was said that 'at one time it was thought that armies could not long stand the fire of smokeless powder on a battlefield, because of the penetrating "chemical" smell it evolved'.[123] Despite playing down this odour, cordite retained its own smell. This mingled with the smell of lubricants on rifles. For example, in the Second

---

[120] Michael Moynihan (ed.), *A Place Called Armageddon: Letters from the Great War* (London: David and Charles, 1975), p. 96.
[121] Siegfried Sassoon, *Memoirs of an Infantry Officer* (London: Faber and Faber, 1930), p. 34.
[122] *Treatise on Ammunition* (London: HM Stationary Office, 1915), p. 32.
[123] Oscar Guttman, 'The Manufacture of Smokeless Powder', *The Journal of the Society of Chemical Industry*, 3:2 (1894), p. 58.

Boer War a junior British Officer described 'the smell of powder (cordite) and the hot oily smell of his rifle'.[124]

Novels written by soldiers who had been in the trenches evoked the smell of cordite as the atmosphere of battle being joined. In H. C. McNeile's 1917 *No Man's Land* fighting starts with a bang as 'the acrid smell of cordite drifted over them, while without cessation there came the solemn boom- boom- boom of the heavier guns way back'.[125] It is possible that in some extreme examples, the smell of gunpowder and cordite lingers in the landscape. In November 2021, a German First World War tunnel was discovered in Northern France that had been left untouched since the end of the conflict. One of the archaeologists involved in assessing the tunnel noted that 'there is the very particular odour of the battlefield because the smell of gunpowder still lingers'.[126] If we were seeking to represent the shifting smell of European warfare more generally we might be interested in representing the shift from gunpowder to cordite, but if we were interested in evoking the smell of the trenches then cordite was an odour that leapt forth from the more constant 'trench atmosphere' of chloride of lime and dead bodies when fighting erupted.

Whilst cordite was a smell characteristic of conflicts from the late nineteenth century to the mid-twentieth century, another odour associated with weaponry was not: gas warfare. There is a rich assortment of fumes and vapours used for their smells and health impacts on combatants that reach back into the seventeenth century and before. In the 1840s there were suggestions that poisonous substances (in this case cacodyl, 'kacodyl' named for its abominable smell, or 'Cadet's fuming liquid') could be weaponized for their awful smell and fatal atmospheric effects.[127] Around 1900 Hiram Maxim (of Maxim machine gun fame) also proposed the use of bombs that would 'emit a suffocating odour so as to force a hasty retreat'.[128] However, the First

---

[124] Nicholas Murray, *The Rocky Road to the Great War* (Dulles: University of Nebraska Press, 2013), p. 111.
[125] H. C. McNeile, *No Man's Land* (London: George H. Doran, 1917), p. 103.
[126] Emma Morgan, 'Rediscovered WW1 Tunnel in France "still smells of gunpowder"', https://www.connexionfrance.com/French-news/Rediscovered-WW1-tunnel-in-Oise-in-northern-France-still-smells-of-gunpowder [accessed 02/11/21].
[127] John Coffern, *Projectile Weapons of War and Explosive Compounds* (London: Longman, 1859), pp. 60–2.
[128] 'The Month; Science and Arts', *Chambers Journal* (1900), p. 495.

World War was the moment when chemical warfare came into its own: in particular the use of phosgene, mustard gas and chlorine gas.

Peter Sloterdijk has claimed that the moment when the Germans deployed chlorine gas on the 22nd April 1915 at Ypres marked the birth of twentieth-century modernity: when mankind shifted from an interest in regulating the body to manipulating, attacking, and controlling the air, the environment, and the conditions of life itself.[129] Earlier writers had imagined the capacity of poisonous, gaseous, clouds to destroy entire populations. For example, in M. P. Shiel's 1901 novel, *The Purple Cloud*, a deadly cloud smelling of almond or peaches covers the earth and destroys human and animal life. These were the same smells of arsenic and cyanide that would also accompany later uses of gas as a weapon of war.[130] Of the gases used in the First World War, phosgene was said to smell like silage, mustard gas like garlic or English mustard and chlorine gas like ammonia or bleach. In his novel *Storm of Steel*, Ernst Jünger describes the 'penetrating' smell of chlorine gas and the 'sweetish' smell of phosgene.[131] Repeated exposure to some weaponized gases, such as cyanoarsine, could dull the smell and therefore deprive soldiers of one of the few ways they had of detecting an oncoming gas assault or leave soldiers with a perpetual and long-lasting fear of any strong smells – even strong smells of flowers.[132]

The response to gas warfare also created its own odours. The gas masks that were deployed in response varied in construction and materials depending on the nation deploying them and the stage of the war. The experience of wearing a gas mask would include, depending on the model since each major combatant used different designs, the smells of leather, rubber and cloth. Gauze soaked in urine was also deployed to protect the body. Gas masks themselves were coated in chemicals. British 'hypo' masks were coated in sodium hyposulphite. The chemical smell of the masks caused wearers to fear they were being poisoned and led them to remove them, resulting in more deaths from the gas attack swirling around them. Checking for lingering gas in a trench involved lifting one's mask and sniffing the air, but these

---

[129] For a shorter version of his argument see Peter Sloterdijk, *Terror from the Air* (Cambridge, MA: MIT Press, 2009).
[130] M. P. Shiel, *The Purple Cloud* (London: University of Nebraska Press, 2000), pp. 54, 61.
[131] Ernst Jünger, *Storm of Steel*, trans. Michael Hoffman (London: Penguin, 2003), pp. 79, 83.
[132] L. F. Haber, *The Poisonous Cloud: Chemical Warfare in the First World War* (Oxford: Oxford University Press, 1986).

atmospheric diagnostics were severely limited by the smell of the mask and the odours of decomposing corpses.[133] As the lingering nature of gas suggests, in seeking to evoke the smell of trench warfare we have to reckon with its temporality. Chemical odours emerged out of the broader trench atmosphere and provided a warning to troops to mask up and prepare for the clouds of strangely coloured gas moving over the trenches.[134] But it is also a smell that might recede as the gas damaged the nose and impaired the ability to detect atmospheric change.

Finally, there are some scents which evoke highly specific moments within a battle and that would modulate in and out of existence in our scent reconstruction in very brief moments. One example here is the smell of rum. In order to give them courage before going 'over the top', some British troops were issued with strong, dark, government rum, and the same rum was administered to the wounded or dying to ease their pain, leading one soldier to remember 'the smell of rum and blood' as the olfactory signature of an attack.[135] However at the other temporal extreme there are, of course, the odours of battlefields that have only emerged in the longer aftermath of the First World War's official end. In 1975, Paul Fussell was still able to write, of the battlefields of the First World War, that 'when the air is damp you can smell the rusted iron everywhere, even though you see only wheat and barley'.[136] This dry-down would linger on in our olfactory interpretation.

Any means of conveying an argument about the past in an olfactory form would have to engage with widely differing temporalities and geographies of odours. There are certain odours which seem omnipresent in multiple times and places. There are others which erupt into the foreground and only gain their significance at particular moments or when linked to particular events. A scent may convey a century of continuity – such as the smell of death or a rupture of time lasting mere minutes or seconds – such as the intoxicating scent of dark rum – and it may evoke a whole neighbourhood or a particular spot on a particular street on a particular morning. What is interesting

---

[133] Tim Cook, *No Place to Run: The Canadian Corps and Gas Warfare in the First World War* (Vancouver: UBC Press, 2011), pp. 58, 68, 85.
[134] U.S Army War College, *Specimens of the British Trench Orders* (Washington, 1917), p. 31.
[135] Paul Fussell, *The Great War and Modern Memory* (Oxford: Oxford University Press, 1975), p. 50.
[136] Ibid., p. 75.

is how these times may converge, as scents converge, in a palimpsestic moment. Perfume therefore offers a powerful way of representing these moments of temporal and spatial evocation. It may yet offer humanities scholars creative, engaging and intellectually nuanced ways of representing and presentifying the past.

Conclusion: Nose-first

By way of conclusion, I want to circle back to one of the first discussions of the desirability or possibility of a history of smells. In 1705, an English translation of Bernadino Ramazzini's *Treatise of the Diseases of Tradesmen* was published in English. In this work, originally published in 1700 in Latin, Ramazzini mentioned his idea for a history of odours, whilst admitting that he did not have the time or space to pursue it. Moyse's depiction of 2nd Gentleman and his quest to understand Shakespeare through smell in his 1889 *Falstaff's Nose*, discussed in the second chapter of this book, had been satirical and the humour had proceeded from the highly improbable method and its results. But Ramazzini was absolutely serious about the desirability and possibility of a history of odours.

What distinguished the two was that Ramazzini was living in an early modern world before the evolution of distinct academic disciplines in the nineteenth century. Ramazzini imagined his history drawing on everything from medicine, science and philosophy to proto-anthropology, religion and the study of past texts. This history of odours would, according to Ramazzini, comprehend 'in one performance whatever lies scatter'd in Authors, or is still to be discover'd by Experiments'.[1] Moyse was writing at the end of the nineteenth century when academic disciplines were coagulating and concretizing into their modern form. In his play the attempts of 2nd Gentleman to bring together the scatterings of the archive with experimental knowledge was to be mocked as the mark of an obsession that transgressed the boundaries of literary historical practice. To some extent perhaps historical research has lost the capacious sense of interrelatedness that characterized the early modern

---

[1] Bernadino Ramazzini, *A Treatise of the Diseases of Tradesmen* (London: Andrew Bell, 1705), p. 96.

production of knowledge. The preceding discussion has providing ample support for the argument that we should recapture that spirit.

In short, this small book has argued the following. The introduction observed the odd situation that scholars interested in smell's past find themselves in. On the one hand, they emphasize the crucial importance of smell to understand the past and on the other they reject the idea that using our noses can in fact be a useful scholarly practice. The first chapter therefore made the case for using our noses as research tools for articulating the past. This involves understanding our own olfactory subjectivities alongside those that came before us and re-odorizing our archives with odours that are only implicit in or obscured by the historical record. The process of understanding our own perceptual habits, re-engaging with past modes of sniffing, and reconstructing or sniffing past materialities in the present is not a process of naively replaying the past but a means of registering differences that help us better understand the olfactory worlds of the past, present and future. It means re-odorizing the materials which we use as scholars and recognizing the implicit odours that may not be expressed in textual archives but nonetheless may have had – continue to have – a significant impact on our olfactory worlds. Registering the odours that evade textual capture will help us read better for implicit smells by enlarging our understanding of the affordances, presences and atmospheres which are or have not been meaning themselves but which are the context in which meaning is created or evoked. Finally, the first chapter argued that the concerns of the present demand a greater engagement with scent. Smell offers a potent means for communicating the need for political or social change in ways that are at once both profoundly intellectual and viscerally emotive. Smell therefore offers a powerful means for communicating research about environmental degradation and global inequalities. The politics of academic knowledge-making and the roots of disciplines in a colonial past that often dismissed non-European epistemologies should force us to reconsider the relationship between our research and the sensate. Decolonizing our practice means challenging our assumptions about disciplinary distributions of the sensible: the rules about what can or cannot be legitimately sensed as part of our work.

The second chapter has explored archives of smell and how to 'read' them. Starting with a nineteenth-century vision of 'nose-on' research, it traces how

Conclusion: Nose-first 119

smell was effaced from humanities methodologies. Our unwillingness to think both with and beyond the human nose – to more-than-human and machine forms of smelling – has obscured the scents we might find in the archives. The historical mediatization of smell – the development of ideas about the extraction and synthesis of scents – has also ended up making smell seem more evanescent, abstract and difficult to archive either in bottles or words. The library and archive have been imagined as either deodorized spaces for thinking or romanticized spaces in which the smell of old books predominates. Despite this, as the chapter went on to suggest, there are plenty of ways in which we can use innovative interdisciplinary methods to better understand the explicit and implicit olfactory archives of the past: from re-odorizing historical spaces to extracting the volatile organic compounds from historical sites and objects and from digitally modelling the dispersal of odours to remaking recipes for historical creations from original instructions. Archives of smell exist – from perfume libraries to volatile organic compounds emitted by historical objects – and there are interesting interdisciplinary tools that can help us uncover them.

Finally, the last chapter has examined the narratives and temporalities of smell we evoke in our scholarly dissemination. It begins with the observation that smell has a peculiar relationship with temporality. Through the example of early modern attempts to stage smell in theatres and their use as a prophylactic, the chapter outlined smell's palimpsestic quality: its ability to compress multiple overlapping times and pasts, presents and futures into a single experience. In order to explore this understanding of smell the chapter then offered a new reading of ideas about 'deodorization' that have become so central to scholarship on smell and its pasts. It argued that deodorization as a practice invokes past, present and future together: it creates stories about smell's histories that emphasize alternatively progress or stagnation, it attempts to alter olfactory atmospheres in the present, and in doing so it creates both anticipations of the very scents it tries to hide and pushes the mirage of total deodorization ever further into the future. Having explored the temporalities of scent, I then argued for an archaeology of odours that takes the molecular materiality of smells seriously as an archive that can be re-connected with meanings in the present. The chapter then made the case for representing historical narratives and arguments through a structured olfactory experience, drawing on the stories evoked via the art of perfumery. Smell – in particular the kinds of constructed scents found in perfumery and olfactory art – can offer a potent way for us to represent and presentify the past.

The central argument in each section of this book has been that our understanding of the past and its relationship with the present is enriched by opening our minds and deploying our – and other more-than-human – noses. In order to make best use of such tools we must also revise our understanding of the temporalities implied by smell and olfactory experience.

Exploring further how this would work in practice will be difficult. However, it is necessary work that is worth the effort because it will force – indeed is already forcing – scholars to interrogate some of their key assumptions about what the study of 'the past' should, can or will look like in the future. Earlier in this book, I claimed that historians have never used smell as a positive metaphor for their research practice. This is not quite correct. The *Annales* school of history that emerged in 1920s and 1930s France comprised the first academic historians to really take the history of feeling seriously. Lucien Febvre wrote an essay on how historians could reconstitute the 'emotional life' of the past and Marc Bloch produced a masterwork on the royal touch – the pre-modern idea that the touch of the monarch could heal the condition of scrofula.[2] Both historians were advocates of a total history that would be geographically, temporally and methodologically capacious. But they also advocated a focus on mentalities and perceptions. Above all, Bloch argued, historians were interested in humans. In his guide to historical research, *The Historian's Craft*, Bloch argued:

> The good historian is like the giant of the fairy tale. He knows that wherever he catches the scent of human flesh, there his quarry lies.[3]

However, in this passage smell is still damned with faint praise. In this invocation of smell the historian is compared to the monstrous and fantastical forms that stalk the boundaries of the human. Today the historian no longer

---

[2] Lucien Febvre, 'Sensibility and History: How to Reconstitute the Emotional Life of the Past,' in Peter Burke (ed.), *A New Kind of History: From the Writings of Febvre*, trans. K. Folca (New York: Routledge, 1973), pp. 12–26. Marc Bloch, *The Royal Touch: Sacred Monarchy and Scrofula in England and France*, trans. J. E. Anderson (London: Routledge, 1973).

[3] Marc Bloch, *The Historian's Craft*, trans. Peter Putnam (Manchester: Manchester University Press, 1992), p. 22.

takes the 'human' as an uncomplicated category of analysis. Histories of bodies, animals, technologies, objects and environments have all led historians to problematize humans and humanity. Any history of feeling is partly a history of how the category of the human has been defined, delimited and policed.[4] By using all of the senses – including our noses – we can better subject the methods of enquiry and presentation in the humanities to the same critical attention as their erstwhile quarry.

If this book is anything it is a call to noses. It asks researchers to wake up and smell not just the coffee, but the whole molecular world that surround us. On first sniff smell may seem ephemeral, mysterious and difficult to describe. But the more we use our noses the more we can remedy those difficulties by noticing the echoes and rhymes of the scents around us, the causes and processes from which odours flow, and the multiple different languages and forms of appreciation that *can* be leveraged to understand our olfactory environments and, indeed, *have* been used to comprehend past atmospheres.

To do so means investing in a new form of smell studies with a different approach to the past. In an 1837 chapter on the 'permanent impression' of 'words and actions' on the 'globe we inhabit' Charles Babbage mused that 'the air itself is one vast library' of both words spoken and the 'acts we have done'.[5] The atmospheres we smell and breathe contain a collection of odorants that we borrow from, interrogate and add meaning to, at the same time as they are supplemented by new molecular deposits or diminished by deodorizing de-accessioning. The olfactory past is not simply *in* the past, separated from us by a vast sensory gulf, but present within and between us as dispositions towards smell that are the product of historical habits. Every sniff is dependent on what is and what is not in the air around us, of what we are able and are not able to recognize or describe, and therefore is linked not only – as Proust would have it – to the 'vast structure of recollection' but to historical and contemporary socio-material processes. A critical smell studies starts at the tip of the nose. So let's follow it.

---

[4] Rob Boddice and Mark Smith, *Emotion, Sense, Experience* (Cambridge: Cambridge University Press, 2020).
[5] Charles Babbage, *The Ninth Bridgewater Treatise* (London: John Murray, 1837), pp. 113–15.

Bibliography

Abraham Hart, Ernest, *An Account of the Condition of the Infirmaries of London Workhouses* (London: Chapman and Hall, 1866).

Ahnfelt, Nils-Otto, Hjalmar Fors and Karin Wendin, 'Historical Continuity or Different Sensory Worlds? What We Can Learn about the Sensory Characteristics of Early Modern Pharmaceuticals by Taking Them to a Trained Sensory Panel', *Berichte zur Wissenschafts-Geschichte*, 43:3 (2020), pp. 412–29.

Albrecht, Felix, 'Between Boon and Bane: The Use of Chemical Reagents in Palimpsest Research in the Nineteenth Century', in M. J. Driscoll (ed.), *Care and Conservation of Manuscripts 13: Proceedings of the Thirteenth International Seminar Held at the University of Copenhagen 13th–15th April 2001* (Copenhagen: Museum Tusculanum Press, 2012), pp. 147–65.

Allen, Louisa, 'The Smell of Lockdown: Smellwalks as Sensuous Methodology', *Qualitative Research*, doi: 10.1177/14687941211007663.

Almagor, Uri, 'Odors and Private Language: Observations on the Phenomenology of Scent', *Human Studies*, 13:3 (1990), pp. 253–74.

Armstrong, Robert G., 'The Smell of Air Pollution: Olfactory Senses and the Odour of Canadian Oil, 1858–1885', *Ontario History*, 112:2 (2020), pp. 211–29.

Baker, Nicholas, *Double Fold: Libraries and the Assault on Paper* (London: Vintage, 2002).

Balez, Suzel, 'Smell Walks', in E. Barbara, A. Piga, et al. (eds.), *Experiential Walks for Urban Design: Revealing, Representing, and Activating the Sensory Environment* (Cham: Springer, 2021), pp. 93–114.

Bann, Stephen, *The Inventions of History: Essays on the Representation of the Past* (Manchester: Manchester University Press, 1990).

Barclay, Katie, 'Falling in Love with the Dead', *Rethinking History*, 22:4 (2018), pp. 459–73.

Barnes, David S., 'Confronting Sensory Crisis in the Great Stinks of London and Paris', in William A. Cohen and Ryan Johnson (eds.), *Filth, Dirt, Disgust and Modern Life* (Minneapolis: University of Minnesota Press, 2004), pp. 103–30.

Barnes, David S., *The Great Stink of Paris and the Nineteenth-century Struggle against Filth and Germs* (Baltimore: Johns Hopkins University Press, 2018).

Baron, Russel T., *A Hundred Years Hence: The Expectations of an Optimist* (London: T. Fisher Unwin, 1905).

Barr, John, *The Assault on Our Senses* (London: Methuen, 1970).

Barthes, Roland, *Sade, Fourier, Loyola*, trans. Richard Miller (Berkeley: University of California Press, 1989).

Barwich, Ann-Sophie, *Smellosophy: What the Nose Tells the Mind* (London: Harvard University Press, 2020).

Barwich, Ann-Sophie and Matthew Rodriguez, 'Fashion Fades, Chanel No.5 Remains: Epistemology between Style and Technology', *Berichte zur Wissenschaftsgeschichte*, 43:3 (2020), pp. 367–84.

Bate, John, *Six Thousand Illustrations of Moral and Religious Truths* (London: Jarrold & Sons, 1885).

Baum, Jacob M., 'From Incense to Idolatry: The Reformation of Olfaction in Late Medieval German Ritual', *The Sixteenth Century Journal*, 44:2 (2013), pp. 323–44.

Beddoes, Thomas, *Essay on the Causes, Early Signs, and Prevention of Pulmonary Consumption for the Use of Parents and Preceptors* (Bristol: Longman and Rees, 1799).

Bedini, Silvio A., 'The Scent of Time. A Study of the Use of Fire and Incense for Time Measurement in Oriental Countries', *Transactions of the American Philosophical Society*, 53:5 (1963), pp. 1–51.

Bellamy, Edward, *Equality* (London: Heinemann, 1897).

Bellamy, Edward, *Looking Backwards from 2000 to 1887* (Boston: Ticknor & Co., 1888).

Bembibre Cecilia, Siobhan Barratt, Luciano Vera, Matija Strlič, 'Smelling the Past: A Case Study for Identification, Analysis and Archival of Historic Potpourri as a Heritage Smell', in J. Bridgland (ed.), *ICOM-CC 18th Triennial Conference Preprints*, Copenhagen, 4–8 September 2017, art. 1601. Paris: International Council of Museums, 2017.

Bembibre, Cecilia, 'Archiving the Intangible: Preserving Smells, Historic Perfumes and Other Ways of Approaching the Scented Past', in Adeline Grand-Clément, et al. (eds.), *The Smells and Senses of Antiquity in the Modern Imagination* (London: Bloomsbury, 2022), pp. 155–73.

Bembibre, Cecilia and Matija Strlič, 'Smell of Heritage: A Framework for the Identification, Analysis and Archival of Historic Odours', *Heritage Science*, 5:2 (2017), pp. 1–11.

Berenstein, Nadia, 'Flavor Added: The Sciences of Flavor and the Industrialization of Taste in America', PhD thesis, University of Pennsylvania, 2017.

Berridge, Virginia and Suzanne Taylor (eds.), *The Big Smoke: Fifty Years after the 1952 London Smog* (London: Centre for History in Public Health, London School of Hygiene and Tropical Medicine, 2005).

Besant, Walter, *London: After the Romans. Saxon and Norman. Plantagenet* (London: Heinemann and Balestier, 1893).

Bevernage, Berber, *History, Memory and State-Sponsored Violence: Time and Justice* (London: Routledge, 2011).

Birdsall, Carolyn, J. F. Missfelder, D. Morat and C. Schleif, 'Forum: The Senses', *German History*, 32:2 (2014), pp. 256–8.

Blair, D., 'The Memory of Smells', *Notes and Queries*, 4th Series, VII, 18 May (1871), p. 413.

Bland, John Otway Percy, *China, Japan, Korea* (London: C. Scribner Sons, 1921).

Bloch, Marc, *The Royal Touch: Sacred Monarchy and Scrofula in England and France*, trans. J. E. Anderson (London: Routledge, 1973).

Bloch, Marc, *The Historian's Craft*, trans. Peter Putnam (Manchester: Manchester University Press, 1992).

Boddice, Rob and Mark Smith, *Emotion, Sense, Experience* (Cambridge: Cambridge University Press, 2020).

Boyd, William, *The Slain Wood: Papermaking and Its Environmental Consequences in the American South* (Baltimore: Johns Hopkins University Press, 2015).

Bradley, Mark, '"It All Comes out in the Wash": Looking Harder at the Roman Fullonica', *Journal of Roman Archaeology*, 15 (2002), pp. 20–44.

Bradstreet, Christina, '*A Trip to Japan in Sixteen Minutes*: Sadakichi Hartmann's Perfume Concert and the Aesthetics of Scent', in Patrizia Di Bello and Gabriel Koureas (eds.), *Art, History and the Senses* (Farnham: Ashgate, 2010), pp. 51–66.

Brant, Clare, 'Fume and Perfume: Some Eighteenth-century Uses of Smell', *Journal of British Studies*, 43:4 (2004), pp. 444–63.

Brant, Clare, 'Scenting a Subject: Odour Poetics and the Politics of Space', *Ethnos*, 73:4 (2008), pp. 544–63.

Brazinski, Paul A. and Allegra R. P. Fryxell, 'The Smell of Relics: Authenticating Saintly Bones and the Role of Scent in the Sensory Experience of Medieval Christian Veneration', *Papers from the Institute of Archaeology*, 23:1 (2013), pp. 1–15.

Brown, John Seeley and Paul Duguid, *The Social Life of Information* (Boston, MA: Harvard University Press, 2017).

Bulliqui, Eddie, 'The Phenomenon of Olfactory Time', https://scentculture.institute/the-phenomenon-of-olfactory-time/#_ftnref93 [accessed 01/03/2022].

Buser, Michael, 'The Time Is Out of Joint: Atmosphere and Hauntology at Bodiam Castle', *Emotion, Space and Society*, 25 (2017), pp. 5–13.

Calkin, Robert R. and J. Stephan Jellinek, *Perfumery: Practice and Principles* (New York: Wiley, 1994).

Campbell, Dr Harry, 'Ventilation of Libraries', *The Lancet*, 20th April 1889, p. 818.

Capelli, Laura, et al., 'Overview of Odour Measurement Methods: The Odour Observatory as an Informative Tool for Citizen Science Based Approaches to Odour Management', *Detritus*, 12 (2020), pp. 169–75.

Carlisle, Clare, *On Habit* (London: Routledge, 2014).
Carr, Edward, *What Is History?* (Basingstoke: Palgrave Macmillan, 2001).
Champion, Matthew S., *The Fullness of Time: Temporalities of the Fifteenth Century* (Chicago: Chicago University Press, 2017).
Chen, Anna, 'Perfume and Vinegar: Olfactory Knowledge, Remembrance, and Recordkeeping', *The American Archivist*, 79:1 (2016), pp. 103–20.
Classen, Constance, 'McLuhan in the Rainforest: The Sensory Worlds of Oral Cultures', in David Howes (ed.), *Empire of the Senses: The Sensual Culture Reader* (London: Routledge, 2005), pp. 147–63.
Classen, Constance, 'Museum Manners: The Sensory Life of the Early Museum', *Journal of Social History*, 40:4 (2007), pp. 895–914.
Coffern, John, *Projectile Weapons of War and Explosive Compounds* (London: Longman, 1859).
Coleridge, Samuel Taylor, *The Works of Samuel Taylor Coleridge, Prose and Verse* (Philadelphia: Thomas Cowperthwait, 1840).
Connor, Steven, 'The Menagerie of the Senses', *Senses and Society*, 1:1 (2006), pp. 9–26.
Conti, Cecilia, et al., 'Measurements Techniques and Models to Assess Odor Annoyance: A Review', *Environment International*, 134 (2020), p. 105261.
Cook, James, *A Voyage towards the South Pole*, 2 vols. (London: W. Strahan and T. Cadell, 1777).
Cooper, Ambrose, *The Complete Distiller* (London: P. Vaillant & R, Griffiths, 1757).
Cooper, Catriona, 'The Sounds of Debate in Georgian England: Auralising the House of Commons', *Parliamentary History*, 38:1 (2019), pp. 60–73.
Corbin, Alain, *The Foul and the Fragrant* (Cambridge: Harvard University Press, 1986).
Corbin, Alain, *Time, Desire, Horror: Towards a History of the Senses* (Cambridge: Polity, 1995).
Corbin, Alain, 'Charting the Cultural History of the Senses', in David Howes (ed.), *Empire of the Senses: The Sensual Culture Reader* (Oxford: Breg, 2005), pp. 128–41.
Corton, Christine L., *London Fog: The Biography* (London: Harvard University Press, 2015).
Crane, Susan A., 'Historical Subjectivity: A Review Essay', *The Journal of Modern History*, 78:2 (2006), pp. 434–56.
Cristani, R. S., *Perfumery and Kindred Arts* (London: Sampson Low, Marston, Searle and Rivington, 1877).
Crowther, Bosley, 'Smells of China; "Behind Great Wall" Uses AromaRama', *The New York Times*, 10th December 1959.
Curran, Katherine, et al., 'Classifying Degraded Modern Polymeric Museum Artefacts by Their Smell', *Angewandte Chemie International Edition*, 57:25 (2018), pp. 7336–40.

Curtis, Bruce, 'I Can Tell by the Way You Smell: Dietetics, Smell, Social Theory', *Senses and Society*, 3:1 (2008), pp. 5–22.

Das, Santanu, *Touch and Intimacy in First World War Literature* (Cambridge: Cambridge University Press, 2005), p. 84.

Davidson, Hilary, 'The Embodied Turn: Making and Remaking Dress as an Academic Practice', *Fashion Theory*, 23:3 (2019), pp. 363–99.

Davies Douglas, J. and Lewis H. Mates (eds.), *Encyclopedia of Cremation* (Farnham: Ashgate, 2005).

de Sousa Santos, Boaventura, *The End of the Cognitive Empire: The Coming of Age of Epistemologies of the South* (Durnham, NC: Duke University Press, 2018).

Dong, Yuanfa, et al., 'Multisensory Virtual Experience of Tanning in Medieval Coventry', *Eurographics Workshop on Graphics and Cultural Heritage* (2017), doi: 10.2312:gch.20171297.

Donkin, Robin A., *Dragon's Brain Perfume: An Historical Geography of Camphor* (Leiden: Brill, 1999).

Drobnick, Jim, 'Preface', in Jim Drobnick (ed.), *The Smell Culture Reader* (Oxford: Berg, 2006), pp. 1–11.

Drobnick, Jim, 'The Museum as Smellscape', in Nina Levent and Alvaro-Pascual-Leone (eds.), *The Multisensory Museum: Cross-disciplinary Perspectives on Touch, Sound, Smell, Memory, and Space* (Lanham, MA: Rowman and Littlefield, 2014), pp. 177–96.

Dugan, Holly, *The Ephemeral History of Perfume: Scent and Sense in Early Modern England* (Baltimore: Johns Hopkin's University Press, 2011).

Dugan, Holly, 'Seeing Smell', in Jackie Watson, et al. (eds.), *The Senses in Early Modern England, 1558–1660* (Manchester: Manchester University Press, 2015), pp. 91–111.

Dumas, Alexander, *The Count of Monte-Cristo* (London: Routledge, 1858).

Dwight, Theodore, *The School-master's Friend, with Committee-man's Guide* (New York: R. Lockwood, 1835).

Ehrich, Sofia, et al., 'Nose-First. Towards an Olfactory Gaze for Digital Art History', *MDK*, 3064 2021.

Ellena, Jean-Claude, *Perfume: The Alchemy of Scent*, trans. John Crisp (New York: Arcade, 2011).

Elliott, John Huxtable, *History in the Making* (London: Yale University Press, 2012).

Erwine, Barbara, *Creating Sensory Spaces: The Architecture of the Invisible* (London: Routledge, 2017).

Eskildsen, Kasper Risbjerg, 'Leopold von Ranke's Archival Turn: Location and Evidence in Modern Historiography', *Modern Intellectual History*, 5:3 (2008), pp. 425–53.

Evans, Joan, *The Unselfish Egoist: A Life of Joseph Joubert* (London: Longman, 1947).
Eve, Stuart, 'A Dead Man's Nose: Using Smell to Explore the Battlefield of Waterloo', in Victoria Henshaw, et al. (eds.), *Designing with Smell: Practices, Techniques, and Challenges* (London: Routledge, 2018), pp. 211–18.
Farge, Arlette, *The Allure of the Archives*, trans. Thomas Scott-Railton (New Haven, CT: Yale University Press, 2013).
Faria, Sandro Felipe Santos, 'Self-Perceived and Self-reported Breath Odour and the Wearing of Face Masks during the COVID-19 Pandemic', *Oral Diseases* (2021), doi: 10.1111/odi.13958.
Febvre, Lucien, 'Sensibility and History: How to Reconstitute the Emotional Life of the Past', in Peter Burke (ed.), *A New Kind of History: From the Writings of Febvre*, trans. K. Folca (New York: Routledge, 1973), pp. 12–26.
Ferranti, Michelle, 'An Odor of Racism: Vaginal Deodorants in African-American Beauty Culture and Advertising', *Advertising & Society Review* (2011), doi: 10.1353/asr.2011.0003.
Fisher, Ruth M., et al., 'Framework for the Use of Odour Wheels to Manage Odours Throughout Wastewater Biosolids Processing', *Science of the Total Environment*, 634 (2018), pp. 214–23.
Fleay, Frederick Gard, *Shakespeare Manual* (London: Macmillan and Company, 1876).
Ford Media Centre, 'Ford Mach Eau', https://media.ford.com/content/fordmedia/feu/en/news/2021/07/14/ford-mach-eau.html [accessed 01/03/2022].
Fors, Hjalmar, et al., 'From the Library to the Laboratory and Back Again: Experiment as a Tool for Historians of Science', *Ambix*, 63:2 (2016), pp. 85–97.
Forster, Johann Reinhold, *Observations Made during a Voyage around the World* (London: G. Robinson, 1778).
Foster, D., et al., 'An Olfactorium', *The American Journal of Psychology*, 10:1 (1950), pp. 431–40.
Fretwell, Erica, *Sensory Experiments: Psychophysics, Race, and the Aesthetics of Feeling* (Durham: Duke University Press, 2020).
Friedman, Emily, *Reading Smell in Eighteenth-century Fiction* (Lewisburg: Bucknell University Press, 2016).
Friedrick, Markus, *The Birth of the Archive: A History of Knowledge* (Ann Arbor: University of Michigan Press, 2018).
Fudge, Erica, 'Milking Other Men's Beasts', *History and Theory*, 52 (2013), pp. 12–28.
Fussell, Paul, *The Great War and Modern Memory* (Oxford: Oxford University Press, 1975).
Gamble, Eleanor Acheson McCulloch, 'The Applicability of Weber's Law to Smell', *The American Journal of Psychology*, 10:1 (1898), pp. 82–142.

Gates Jr., Henry Louis, *Colored People: A Memoir* (London: Penguin, 1995).
Gil Harris, Jonathan, 'The Smell of Macbeth', *Shakespeare Quarterly*, 58:4 (2007), pp. 465–86.
Gilbert, Avery, *What the Nose Knows: The Science of Scent in Everyday Life* (New York: Crown, 2008).
Glennie, Paul and Nigel Thrift, *Shaping the Day: A History of Timekeeping in England and Wales 1300–1800* (Oxford: Oxford University Press, 2009).
Goltzenleuchter, Brian, 'Scenting the Antiseptic Institution', in Victorian Henshaw, et al. (eds.), *Designing with Smell: Practices, Techniques, and Challenges* (London: Routledge, 2018), pp. 248–58.
Greenhough, William H., *On Ventilation, Heating, and Lighting of Free Public Libraries* (Reading, 1890).
Grimshaw, Robert, *Fifty Years Hence, or, What May Be in 1943* (New York: Practical Publishing Co., 1892).
Groes, Sebastian and Tom Mercer, 'Smell and Memory in the Black Country: The Snidge Scrumpin' Experiments', in Sebastian Groes and R. M. Francis (eds.), *Smell, Memory, and Literature in the Black Country* (Basingstoke: Palgrave Macmillan, 2021), pp. 59–80.
Groom, Nigel, *New Perfume Handbook* (London: Chapman and Hall, 1992).
Gubbins, Herbert, *The Elixir of Life: Or, 2905 A.D.; a Novel of the Far Future* (London: H. J. Drane, 1914).
Guldi, Jo and David Armitage, *The History Manifesto* (Cambridge: Cambridge University Press, 2014).
Gumbrecht, Hans Ulrich, *The Production of Presence: What Meaning Cannot Convey* (Stanford: Stanford University Press, 2004).
Gurdon, Martin, 'Can Classic Cars Go Electric?' https://www.spectator.co.uk/article/can-classic-cars-go-electric- [accessed 01/03/2022].
Guttman, Oscar, 'The Manufacture of Smokeless Powder', *The Journal of the Society of Chemical Industry*, (1894), pp. 575–84.
Haber, Ludwig Fritz, *The Poisonous Cloud: Chemical Warfare in the First World War* (Oxford: Oxford University Press, 1986).
Hamilakis, Yannis, *Archaeology and the Senses: Human Experience, Memory and Affect* (Cambridge: Cambridge University Press, 2014).
Hamilton, Paul, 'The Proust Effect: Oral History and the Senses', in Donald A. Ritchie (ed.), *The Oxford Handbook of Oral History* (Oxford: Oxford University Press, 2012), pp. 219–32.
Hammond, Adam, *Literature in the Digital Age* (Cambridge: Cambridge University Press, 2016).

Han, Byung-Chul, *Scent of Time: A Philosophical Essay on the Art of Lingering*, trans. Daniel Steuer (London: Polity, 2017).

Hanß, Stefan, 'The Fetish of Accuracy: Perspectives on Early Modern Time(s)', *Past and Present*, 243:1 (2019), pp. 267–84.

Harris, Anna, *A Sensory Education* (London: Routledge, 2021).

Harris, Mitchell M., 'The Expense of Ink and Wastes of Shame: Poetic Generation, Black Ink, and Material Waste in Shakespeare's Sonnets', in Andrea Feeser, et al. (eds.), *The Materiality of Color: The Production, Circulation, and Application of Dyes and Pigments, 1400–1800* (Farnham: Ashgate, 2012), pp. 65–80.

Hartman, George, *The Family Physician* (London: R. Wellington, 1696).

Harvey, Elizabeth D., 'Affect, Perfume, and Early Modern Sensory Boundaries', *Resilience: A Journal of the Environmental Humanities*, 5:3 (2018), pp. 31–50.

Haunted Man, A., 'Every-Day Ghosts', *The English Woman's Journal*, 5:30 (1860), pp. 37–40.

Hawkesworth, John, *Account of the Voyages*, 3 vols. (London: W. Strahan and T. Cadell, 1773).

Heathcote, Graham, 'Museum Offers Sights, Sounds, and Smells of World War I Trench', https://apnews.com/article/9b9f2bd201ccc751e774ba98f9f18f7b [accessed 02/11/2021].

Hegel, G. W. F., *Aesthetics. Lectures on Fine Art*, trans. Thomas Malcolm Knox, 2 vols. (Oxford: Clarendon Press, 1998).

Henshaw, Victoria, *Urban Smellscapes: Understanding and Designing City Smell Environments* (London: Routledge, 2014).

Hertodt, Johann Ferdinand, *Crocologia: A Detailed Study of Saffron, the King of Plants*, trans. Sally Francis and Maria Teresa Ramandi (Leiden: Brill, 2020).

Hertz, Rachel S., 'I Know What I Like: Understanding Odor Preferences', in Jim Drobnick (ed.), *The Smell Culture Reader* (Oxford: Berg, 2006), pp. 190–206.

Hesketh, Ian, 'Writing History in Macaulay's Shadow: J. R. Seeley, E. A. Freeman, and the Audience for Scientific History in Late Victorian Britain', *Journal of the Canadian Historical Association*, 22:2 (2011), pp. 30–56.

Hickman, Clare, 'Pine Fresh: The Cultural and Medical Context of Pine Scent in Relation to Health—from the Forest to the Home', *Medical Humanities*, 48:1 (2022), pp. 104–13.

Historians for Future, 'Statement', https://historiansforfuture.org/statement/ [accessed 25/01/2022].

Holden, Michael, 'Norfolk's Bure Valley Railway Tests New Bio-coal for Steam Locomotives', https://www.railadvent.co.uk/2021/06/norfolks-bure-valley-railway-tests-new-bio-coal-for-steam-locomotives.html [accessed 01/03/2022].

Hölscher, Lucian, 'Mysteries of Historical Order: Ruptures, Simultaneity, and the Relationship of the Past, Present, and Future', in Chris Lorenz and Berber Bevernage (eds.), *Breaking up Time: Negotiating the Borders between Past, Present and Future* (Göttingen: Vandenhoeck and Ruprehct, 2013), pp. 134–53.

Holtorf, Cornelius, 'The Presence of Pastness: Themed Environments and Beyond', in Carolyn Oesterle, et al. (eds.), *Staging the Past: Themed Environments in Transcultural Perspective* (Bielefeld: Transcript Verlag, 2014), pp. 23–40.

Howes, David, 'Olfaction and Transition: An Essay on the Ritual Uses of Smell', *Canadian Review of Sociology*, 24:3 (1987), pp. 398–416.

Howes, David, Constance Classen and Anthony Synnott, *Aroma: The Cultural History of Smell* (London: Routledge, 1994).

Hsu, Hsuan, *The Smell of Risk: Environmental Disparities and Olfactory Aesthetics* (New York: New York University Press, 2020).

Humphrey, Grace, *Poland, the Unexplored* (Indianapollis: The Bobbs-Merrill Company, 1931).

Hunter-Crawley, Heather, 'Classical Archaeology and the Senses: A Paradigmatic Shift?', in Robin Keates and Jo Day (eds.), *The Routledge Handbook of Sensory Archaeology* (Abingdon: Routledge, 2019), pp. 434–50.

Hurst, Steve, 'The Senses: Battlefield Exploration, Drawing and Sculpture', in Nicholas J. Saunders and Paul Cornish (eds.), *Modern Conflict and the Senses* (London: Routledge, 2017), pp. 344–60.

Hyde, Alan, *Bodies of Law* (Princeton: Princeton University Press, 1997).

IFF, 'Fragrance Ingredients Compendium', https://www.iff.com/portfolio/products/fragrance-ingredients/online-compendium [accessed 23/02/2021].

Jenkins, Jennifer, 'Archiving the Ephemeral Experience', in Karen F. Gracy (ed.), *Emerging Trends in Archival Science* (London: Rowman and Littlefield, 2018), pp. 77–94.

Jenner, Mark, 'Civilization and Deodorization? Smell in Early Modern English Culture', in Peter Burke, et al. (eds.), *Civil Histories* (Oxford: Oxford University Press, 2000), pp. 127–44.

Jenner, Mark, 'Follow Your Nose? Smell, Smelling, and Their Histories', *American Historical Review*, 116:2 (2011), pp. 335–51.

Jenner, Mark, 'Tasting Lichfield, Touching China: Sir John Floyer's Senses', *The Historical Journal*, 53:3 (2010), pp. 647–70.

Jeurgens, Charles, 'The Scent of the Digital Archive: Dilemmas with Archive Digitisation', *Bijdragen En Mededelingen Betreffende de Beschiendenis der Nederlanden*, 128:4 (2013), pp. 30–54.

Jøgensen, Johanness, *Saint Catherine of Siena* (London: Longman, 1938).

Jones, E. M., C. Overy and E. M. Tansey (eds.), *Air Pollution Research in Britain c.1955–c.2000*, Wellcome Witnesses to Contemporary Medicine, vol. 58 (London: Queen Mary University of London, 2016).

Jørgensen, Dolly, 'The Medieval Sense of Smell, Stench, and Sanitation', in Ulrike Krampl, et al. (eds.), *Les cinq sens de la ville du Moyen âge à nos jours* (Tours: Presses Universitaires Francois-Rabelais, 2013), pp. 301–13.

Julius Le Moyne, F., *Cremation. An Argument* (Pittsburgh: E.W. Lightner, 1878).

Jünger, Ernst, *Storm of Steel*, trans. Michael Hoffman (London: Penguin, 2003).

Jury, Louise, 'Whiff of Almond Falls Victim to Terror Alert', *The Independent*, Thursday 14th November 2002, https://www.independent.co.uk/news/media/whiff-of-almond-falls-victim-to-terror-alert-133417.html [accessed 25/01/2022].

Kant, Immanuel, *Anthropology from a Pragmatic Point of View*, (eds.), Robert B. Louden and Manfred Kuehn (Cambridge: Cambridge University Press, 2006).

Keates, Robin and Jo Day (eds.), *The Routledge Handbook of Sensory Archaeology* (Abingdon: Routledge, 2019).

Keller, Andreas, 'The Scented Museum', in Nina Levent and Alvaro Pascual-Leone (eds.), *The Multisensory Museum: Cross-disciplinary Perspectives on Touch, Sound, Smell, Memory, and Space* (Lanham, MA: Rowman and Littlefield, 2014), pp. 167–76.

Kettler, Andrew, 'Delightful a Fragrance: Native American Olfactory Aesthetics within the Eighteenth-century Anglo American Botanical Community', in Daniela Hacke and Paul Musselwhite (eds.), *Empire of the Senses: Sensory Practices of Colonialism in Early America* (Leiden: Brill, 2018), pp. 223–54.

Kettler, Andrew, '"Ravishing Odors of Paradise": Jesuits, Olfaction, and Seventeenth-century North America', *Journal of American Studies* 50:4 (2016), pp. 827–52.

Kettler, Andrew, *The Smell of Slavery: Olfactory Racism and the Atlantic World* (Cambridge: Cambridge University Press, 2020).

Kiechle, Melanie, *Smell Detectives: An Olfactory History of Nineteenth-century Urban America* (London: University of Washington Press, 2017).

King, Rachel, '"The Beads with Which We Pray Are Made from It": Devotional Ambers in Early Modern Italy', in Christine Göttler and Wietse de Boer (eds.), *Religion and the Senses in Early Modern Europe* (Leiden: Brill, 2013), pp. 153–76.

Labuhn, Beata, 'Breathing a Moldy Air: Olfactory Experience, Aesthetics, and Ethics in the Writing of Ruskin and Riegl', *Future Anterior: Journal of Historic Preservation, Theory, and Criticism*, 13:2 (2016), pp. 103–17.

Lacey, Kate, *Listening Publics: The Politics and Experience of Listening in the Media Age* (London: Polity, 2013).

Lane Notter, J. and R. H. Firther, *The Theory and Practice of Hygiene* (London: J. & A. Churchill, 1896).

Lange, Britta, 'Archive, Collection, Museum: On the History of the Archiving of Voices at the Sound Archive of the Humboldt University', *Journal of Sonic Studies*, 13 (2017), https://www.researchcatalogue.net/view/326465/326466/0/0 [accessed 22/03/2021].

Laporte, Dominque, *History of Shit*, trans. Nadia Benabid and Rodolphe El-khoury (Cambridge: MIT Press, 2002).

Latour, Bruno, 'How to Talk about the Body? The Normative Dimension of Science Studies', *Body & Society*, 10:2–3 (2004), pp. 205–29.

Lawson, John, *A Voyage to Carolina* (London, 1709).

Layne, D. A., 'A Review on Smog', *Journal of the Royal Society of Health*, 75:2 (1955), pp. 171–92.

Lazakis, Nat, *Body Odor and Biopolitics: Characterizing Smell in Neoliberal America* (New York: McFarland, 2021).

Lazakis, Nat, '"It Is a Non-negotiable Order": Public Libraries' Body Odor Bans and the Ableist Politics of Purity', *Journal of Radical Librarianship*, 6 (2020), pp. 24–52.

Lepecki, Andre, 'The Body as Archive: Will to Re-enact and the Afterlives of Dance', *Dance Research Journal*, 42:2 (2010), pp. 28–48.

Leven, Mark, Penny Roberts and Rob Johnson (eds.), *History at the End of the World? History, Climate Change and the Possibility of Closure* (London: HEB Humanities ebooks, 2010).

Liebelt, Claudia, 'Celebrating the Feast of Sweet Smells and Tastes during Corona Times', *Cultures of Hygiene*, https://culthygiene.hypotheses.org/126 [accessed 13/01/2022].

Lincoln, D. F., 'Ventilation of Libraries', *The Library Journal*, 4 (1879), p. 255.

'A London Board of Health Hunting after Cases like Cholera', 1832, chalk lithograph, 14.2 × 23.7cm, Wellcome Library no. 1998i.

'London a Hundred Years Hence', *The Leisure Hour*, 6 (1857), pp. 701–3.

Lorenzo, Ulla and De La Cruz Redondo, 'Women and Conflict in the Iberian Book Trade, 1472–1700', in Alexander Samuel Wilkinson and Graeme Kemp (eds.), *Negotiating Conflict and Controversy in the Early Modern Book World* (Leiden: Brill, 2019), pp. 129–41.

Lynn, Gwenn-Ael and Debra Riley Parr (eds.), *Olfactory Art and the Political in an Age of Resistance* (London: Routledge, 2021).

Mack, Adam, '"Speaking of Tomatoes": Supermarkets, the Senses, and Sexual Fantasy in Modern America', *Journal of Social History*, 43:4 (2010), pp. 815–42.

Maguire, Laurie E., *Shakespearean Suspect Texts: The 'Bad' Quartos and Their Contexts* (Cambridge: Cambridge University Press, 1996).

Majid, Asifa, 'Human Olfaction at the Intersection of Language, Culture, and Biology', *Trends in Cognitive Sciences*, 25:2 (2021), pp. 111–23.

Majid, Asifa and Stephen C. Levinson, 'The Senses in Language and Culture', *Senses and Society*, 6:1 (2011), pp. 5–18.

Majid, Asifa, et al., 'What Makes a Better Smeller?' *Perception*, 46:3–4 (2017), pp. 406–30.

Manguel, Albert, *The Library at Night* (London: Yale University Press, 2008).

Marbecke, Roger, *A Defence of Tabacco vvith a Friendly Answer to the Late Printed Booke called Worke for Chimny-Sweepers, &c* (London: Richard Field, 1602).

Marks, Laura U., 'Thinking Multisensory Culture', in Francesca Bacci and David Melcher (eds.), *Art and the Senses* (Oxford: Oxford University Press, 2011), pp. 239–50.

Marks, Laura U., *Touch: Sensuous Theory and Multisensory Media* (Minneapolis: University of Minnesota Press, 2002).

Martin, Alexander M., 'Sewage and the City: Filth, Smell, and Representations of Urban Life in Moscow, 1770–1880', *Russian Review*, 67:2 (2008), pp. 243–74.

Martin-Moruno, Dolores and Beatriz Pichel, 'Introduction', in Dolores Martin-Moruno and Beatriz Pichel (eds.), *Emotional Bodies: The Historical Performativity of Emotions* (Chicago: University of Illinois Press, 2019), pp. 1–14.

Matsutake Worlds Research Group, 'Strong Collaboration as a Method for Multi-sited Ethnography: On Mycorrhizal Relations', in Mark-Anthony Falzon (ed.), *Multi-sited Ethnography: Theory, Praxis, and Locality in Contemporary Research* (Farnham: Ashgate, 2009), pp. 197–214.

Mattern, Shannon, 'Field', in Nanna Bonde Thylstrup, et al. (eds.), *Uncertain Archives: Critical Keywords for Big Data* (Cambridge, MA: MIT Press, 2021), pp. 227–35.

Mattern, Shannon, 'Resonant Texts: Sounds of the American Public Library', *Senses and Society*, 2:3 (2007), pp. 277–302.

Maurer, Edward S., *Perfumes and Their Production* (London: United Trade Press, 1958).

Maxwell, Catherine, *Scents and Sensibility: Perfume in Victorian Literary Culture* (Oxford: Oxford University Press, 2017).

May, Robert, *The Accomplisht Cook* (London: R. Wood, 1665).

McCann, Hannah and William Tullett, 'The Pandemic Sensory Archive: Smell', www.archiveofintimacy.com/smell [accessed 13/01/2022].

McClean, Kate, 'Two Centuries of Stink: Widnes', https://sensorymaps.com/?projects=two-centuries-of-stink-widnes [accessed 16/02/2022].

McGann, John P., 'Poor Human Olfaction Is a 19th-century Myth', *Science*, 356:6338 (2017), p. eamm7263.

McGee, Harold, *Nose-dive: A Field Guide to the World's Smells* (London: John Murray, 2020).

McHugh, James, 'Seeing Scents: Methodological Reflections on the Intersensory Perception of Aromatics in South Asian Religions', *History of Religions*, 51:2 (2011), pp. 156–77.

McKitterick, David, *The Invention of Rare Books: Private Interest and Public Memory, 1600–1840* (Cambridge: Cambridge University, 2019).

McLean, Kate, 'Temporalities of the Smellscape: Creative Mapping as Visual Representation', in O. Kühne (eds.), *Modern Approaches to the Visualization of Landscapes* (Weisbaden: Springer, 2020), pp. 217–37.

McNeile, H. C., *No Man's Land* (London: George H. Doran, 1917).

Melchiori, Giorgio (ed.), *The Merry Wives of Windsor* (London: Bloomsbury, 1999).

Miles, Stephen, 'Sensorial Engagement in Tourism Experiences on the Western Front', in Nicholas J. Saunders and Paul Cornish (eds.), *Modern Conflict and the Senses* (London: Routledge, 2017), pp. 76–92.

Millard, C. J., 'Using Personal Experience in the Academic Medical Humanities: A Genealogy', *Social Theory and Health*, 18 (2020), pp. 184–98.

Moffett, Thomas, *Health's Improvement* (London: T. Osborne, 1743).

Montanari, Andrea, 'The Stinky King: Western Attitudes toward the Durian in Colonial Southeast Asia', *Food, Culture and Society*, 20:3 (2017), pp. 395–414.

Morag-Levine, Noga, *Chasing the Wind: Regulating Air Pollution in the Common Law State* (Oxford: Princeton University Press, 2003).

Morgan, Emma, 'Rediscovered WW1 Tunnel in France "still Smells of Gunpowder"', https://www.connexionfrance.com/French-news/Rediscovered-WW1-tunnel-in-Oise-in-northern-France-still-smells-of-gunpowder [accessed 02/11/2021].

Morton, Timothy, *The Poetics of Spice* (Cambridge: Cambridge University Press, 2006).

Morton, Timothy, *Hyperobjects: Philosophy and Ecology after the End of the World* (Minneapolis: University of Minnesota Press, 2013).

Motion, Andrew, *The Poetry of Edward Thomas* (London: Random House, 1980).

Moynihan, Michael (ed.), *A Place Called Armageddon: Letters from the Great War* (London: David and Charles, 1975).

Muniesa, Fabian and Anne-Sophie Trébuchet-Breitwiller, 'Becoming a Measuring Instrument', *Journal of Cultural Economy*, 3:3 (2010), pp. 321–37.

Murray, Lisa, 'Big Smoke Stacks: Competing Memories of the Sounds and Smells of Industrial Heritage', in Joy Damousi and Paula Hamilton (eds.), *A Cultural History of Sound, Memory and the Senses* (London: Routledge, 2017), pp. 179–93.

Murray, Nicholas, *The Rocky Road to the Great War* (Dulles: University of Nebraska Press, 2013).

Neidhart, Christoph, *Russia's Carnival: The Smells, Sights, and Sounds of Transition* (New York: Rowman and Littlefield, 2002).

Newell, Jenny, 'Old Objects, New Media: Historical Collections, Digitization and Affect', *Journal of Material Culture*, 17:3 (2012), pp. 287–306.

Newstead, Sarah and Tânia Manuel Casimiro, 'What's That Smell? New Directions for Materials Studies', *Antiquity*, 94:377 (2020), pp. 1314–24.

Nicolis, Franco, 'The Scent of Snow at Punta Linke: First World War Sites as Sensescapes, Trentino, Italy', in Nicholas J. Saunders and Paul Cornish (eds.), *Modern Conflict and the Senses* (London: Routledge, 2017), pp. 61–75.

Nicoll, Ruaridh, 'Strike a Light, Smokeless Pubs Stink', *The Guardian*, 31st October 2004, https://www.theguardian.com/uk/2004/oct/31/smoking.comment [accessed 11/02/2022].

'Noxious Vapours and Health', *English Mechanic and World of Science*, 28:704 (1878), p. 28.

Norman, Henry, 'Motorists and the Public', *The World's Work*, 2 (1903), p. 124.

O'Fogherty, Tedy, *A Letter from the Revd. Faether [sic] Tedy O'Fogherty to a Count of Milan* (Dublin, 1764).

O'Keefe, Paul, *Waterloo: The Aftermath* (London: Random House, 2014).

'Observations on Pennant's London', *The Gentleman's Magazine*, 68 (1790), p. 612.

Ockerman, Emma, 'Rotten Eggs, Paint, and Garbage: What Environmental Racism Smells Like', *Vice*, 9th December 2021, https://www.vice.com/en/article/7kb8ed/environmental-racism-cause-of-bad-smelling-neighborhoods [accessed 21/01/2022].

Oken, Lorenz, *Elements of Physiophilosophy* (London: Ray Society, 1847).

Olivier, Laurent, 'The Business of Archaeology Is the Present', in Alfredo Gonzalez-Ruibal (ed.), *Reclaiming Archaeology: Beyond the Tropes of Modernity* (London: Routledge, 2013), pp. 117–29.

Pacific Northwest Library Association, *Proceedings of the Annual Conference of the Pacific Northwest Library Association* (Tacoma: Press of the Allen & Lamborn Printing Co., 1928).

Parkinson, Sydney, *Journal of a Voyage to the South Seas* (London: Stanfield Parkinson, 1773).

Parsons, Meg and Karen Fisher, 'Historical Smellscapes in Aotearoa New Zealand: Intersections between Colonial Knowledges of Smell, Race, and Wetlands', *Journal of Historical Geography*, 74 (2021), pp. 28–43.

Pearson, Chris, 'A Walk in the Park with Timmy: History and the Possibilities of Companion Species Research', *The Wild*, 1 (2009), pp. 87–96.

Peck, Bradford, *The World a Department Store: A Story of Life under a Cooperative System* (Boston, 1900).

Perkins, Chris and Kate McLean, 'Smell Walking and Mapping', in Helen Holmes and Sarah Marie Hall (eds.), *Mundane Methods: Innovative Ways to Research the Everyday* (Manchester: Manchester University Press, 2020), pp. 156–73.

Pickett, Holly Crawford, 'The Idolatrous Nose: Incense on the Early Modern Stage', in Jane Hwang Degenhardt and Elizabeth Williamson (eds.), *Religion and Drama in Early Modern England* (Farnham: Ashgate, 2011), pp. 19–38.

Plamper, Jan, 'Sounds of February, Smells of October: The Russian Revolution as Sensory Experience', *American Historical Review*, 126:1 (2021), pp. 140–55.

Platts, Hannah, *Multisensory Living in Ancient Rome: Power and Space in Roman Houses* (London: Bloomsbury, 2019).

Porteous, Douglas J., 'Smellscape', *Progress in Physical Geography*, 9:3 (1985), pp. 356–78.

Porter, Jess, et al., 'Mechanisms of Scent-tracking in Humans', *Nature Neuroscience*, 10 (2007), pp. 27–9.

Poucher William Arthur, 'A Classification of Odours and Its Uses', *Journal of the Society of Cosmetic Chemists*, 6:2(1955), pp. 81–94.

Proust, Marcel, *On Art and Literature, 1896–1919*, trans. Sylvia Townsend Warner (New York: Dell, 1964).

Ramazzini, Bernadino, *A Treatise of the Diseases of Tradesmen* (London: A. Bell, 1705).

Rancière, Jacques, *The Politics of Aesthetics* (London: Bloomsbury, 2013).

Ranke, Leopold von, *History of the Latin and Teutonic Nations (1494–1514)*, trans. G. R. Dennis (London: George Bell and Sons, 1909).

Rawcliffe, Carole, *Urban Bodies: Communal Health in Late Medieval English Towns and Cities* (Woodbridge: Boydell, 2013).

Read, Sophie, 'Ambergris and Early Modern Languages of Scent', *The Seventeenth Century*, 28:2 (2013), pp. 221–37.

Reclus, Elisse, *The Earth and Its Inhabitants, Europe: VI The British Isles* (New York: D. Appleton and Company, 1881).

Reinarz, Jonathan, *Past Scents: Historical Perspectives on Smell* (Chicago: University of Illinois Press, 2014).

Revesz, Richard L. and Jack Lienke, *Struggling for Air: Power Plants and the 'War on Coal'* (Oxford: Oxford University Press, 2016).

Rhys-Taylor, Alex, *Food and Multiculture: A Sensory Ethnography of East London* (London: Bloomsbury, 2017).

Rickman, John, *Journal of Captain Cook's Last Voyage to the Pacific Ocean* (London: E. Newbery, 1781).

Rimmel, Eugene, *The Book of Perfumes* (London: Chapman and Hall, 1865).

Robinson, Emily, 'Touching the Void: Affective History and the Impossible', *Rethinking History*, 14 (2010), pp. 503–20.

Robinson, James Harvey, *Medieval and Modern Times* (Boston: Ginn, 1916).

Robinson, James Harvey, Charles A. Beard and James Henry Breasted, *Outlines of European History,* 2 vols. (Bostin: Ginn, 1914).

Roholm, Kaj, 'The Fog Disaster in the Meuse Valley, 1930: A Fluorine Intoxication', *The Journal of Industrial Hygiene and Toxicology*, 19:3 (1937), pp. 126–37.

Rosslyn Earp, J., 'Odors: Their Sanitary Significance and Their Elimination', *American Journal of Public Health*, 13:4 (1923), pp. 283–93.

Said, Edward, *Orientalism* (London: Penguin, 1995).

Salber Philips, Mark, *On Historical Distance* (London: Yale University Press, 2013).

Salmi, Hannu, *What Is Digital History?* (London: Polity, 2021).

Sanders, Julie, 'Under the Skin: A Neighbourhood Ethnography of Leather and Early Modern Drama', in Rory Loughnane and Edel Semple (eds.), *Staged Normality in Shakespeare's England* (Basingstoke: Palgrave Macmillan, 2018), pp. 109–26.

Sassoon, Siegfried, *Memoirs of an Infantry Officer* (London: Faber and Faber, 1930).

Saunders, Nicholas J., et al. (eds.), *Modern Conflict and the Senses* (London: Routledge, 2017).

Scott, Walter, 'The Field of Waterloo', in *The Poetical Works of Sir Walter Scott* (London: Adam and Charles Black, 1857).

Scripture, Edward Wheeler, *Thinking, Feeling, Doing* (Meadville Penna: Flood and Vincent, 1895).

Sear, Cynthia, 'Porous Bodies', *Anthropology in Action*, 27:2 (2020), pp. 73–7.

Semuels, Alana, 'Our Shopping Obsession Is Causing a Literal Stink', *Time*, 15th December 2021, https://time.com/6127646/box-factories-pollution/ [accessed 21/01/2022].

Shakespeare, William, 'Sonnet 5', in Colin Burrow (ed.), *William Shakespeare: The Complete Sonnets and Poems* (Oxford: Oxford University Press, 2002), p. 138.

Shapin, Steven, 'The Sciences of Subjectivity', *Social Studies of Science*, 42:2 (2012), pp. 170–84.

Shapin, Steven, '"You Are What You Eat": Historical Changes in Ideas about Food and Identity', *Historical Research*, 87:237 (2014), pp. 377–92.

Sheldrake, Merlin, *Entangled Life: How Fungi Make our Worlds, Change Our Minds, and Shape Our Futures* (London: Vintage, 2020).

Shepherd-Barr, Kirsten, '"Mise En Scent": The Theatre d'Art's *Cantique Des Cantiques* and the Use of Smell as a Theatrical Device', *Theatre Research International*, 24:2 (1999), pp. 152–9.

Sherman, Stuart, *Telling Time: Clocks, Diaries, and English Diurnal Form* (Chicago: University of Chicago Press, 1996).

Shiel, Matthew Phipps, *The Purple Cloud* (London: University of Nebraska Press, 2000).

Shiner, Larry, *Art Scents: Exploring the Aesthetics of Smell and the Olfactory Arts* (Oxford: Oxford University Press, 2020).

Skelton, Leona J., *Sanitation in Urban Britain, 1560–1700* (London: Routledge, 2016).

Śliwa, Martyna and Kathleen Riach, 'Making Scents of Transition: Smellscapes and the Everyday in "Old" and "New" Urban Poland', *Urban Studies*, 49:1 (2011), pp. 23–41.

Sloterdijk, Peter, *Terror from the Air* (Cambridge, MA: MIT Press, 2009).

Smith, Eliza, *The Compleat Housewife* (London: R. Ware, 1750).

Smith, Mark, *Listening to Nineteenth-century America* (Chapel Hill: University of North Carolina Press, 2001).

Smith, Mark, 'Producing Sense, Consuming Sense, Making Sense: Perils and Prospects for Sensory History', *Journal of Social History*, 40:4 (2007), p. 841.

Smith, Mark, *Sensing the Past: Seeing, Hearing, Smelling, Tasting, and Touching History* (Berkeley, CA: University of California Press, 2007).

Smith, Mark, 'Transcending, Othering, Detecting: Smell, Premodernity, Modernity', *Postmedieval: A Journal of Medieval Cultural Studies*, 3:4 (2012), pp. 380–90.

Smith, Mark. M., *A Sensory History Manifesto* (University Park: Penn State University Press, 2021).

Smith, Watson, 'Manufacture of Alkalis and Acids', *Transactions of the Sanitary Institute*, XIV (1894), pp. 169–207.

Sobchack, Vivia, 'Afterward: Media Archaeology and Re-presencing the Past', in Erkki Huhtamo and Jussi Parikka (eds.), *Media Archaeology: Approaches, Applications, and Implications* (Berkeley: University of California Press, 2011), pp. 323–34.

'A Sock in the Nose', *Time*, 21st December 1959, p. 57.

Soderholm, Kristina, 'Environmental Awakening in the Swedish Pulp and Paper Industry: Pollution Resistance and Firm Responses in the Early 20th Century', *Business Strategy and the Environment*, 18 (2009), pp. 32–42.

Spackman, Christy and Gary A. Burlingame, 'Sensory Politics: The Tug-of-War between Potability and Palatability in Municipal Water Production', *Social Studies of Science*, 48:3 (2018), pp. 350–71.

Stamelman, Richard Howard, *Perfume Joy, Obsession, Scandal, Sin: A Cultural History of Fragrance from 1750 to the Present* (London: Random House, 2009).

Stanley, William, *The Case of the Fox: Being His Prophecies, under Hypnotism, of the Period Ending A.D. 1950: A Political Utopia* (London: Truslove & Hanson, 1903).

Stearn, Miranda, 'Contemporary Challenges: Artistic Interventions in Museums and Galleries Dealing with Challenging Histories', in Jenny Kidd, et al. (eds.), *Challenging History in the Museum* (London: Routledge, 2016), pp. 101–14.

Stenslund, Annette, 'A Whiff of Nothing: The Atmospheric Absence of Smell', *The Senses and Society*, 10:3 (2015), pp. 341–60.

Sterne, Jonathan, *The Audible Past: Cultural Origins of Sound Reproduction* (Durham, NC: Duke University Press, 2003).

Stevenson, Richard J., 'The Forgotten Sense: Using Olfaction in a Museum Context: A Neuroscience Perspective', in Nina Levent and Alvaro Pascual-Leone (eds.), *The Multisensory Museum: Cross-disciplinary Perspectives on Touch, Sound, Smell, Memory, and Space* (Lanham, MA: Rowman and Littlefield, 2014), pp. 151–66.

Storm, Erica M., 'Gilding the Pill: The Sensuous Consumption of Patent Medicines, 1815–1841', *Social History of Medicine*, 31:1 (2018), pp. 41–60.

Strlič, Matija, et al., 'Material Degradomics: On the Smell of Old Books', *Analytical Chemistry*, 81:20 (2009), pp. 8617–22.

Stubbes, Phillip, *The Anatomie of Absuses* (London: Richard Jones, 1583).

Suominen, Jaakko, Antti Silvast and Tuomas Harviainen, 'Smelling Machine History: Olfactory Experiences of Information Technology', *Technology and Culture*, 59:2 (2018), pp. 313–37.

Takats, Sean, *The Expert Cook in Enlightenment France* (Baltimore: Johns Hopkins University Press, 2011).

Tamm, Marek and Laurent Olivier, 'Introduction: Rethinking Historical Time', in Marek Tamm and Laurent Olivier (eds.), *Rethinking Historical Time* (London: Bloomsbury, 2019), pp. 1–22.

Thompson, C. J. S., *The Mystery and Lure of Perfume* (London: John Lane, 1927).

Thompson, Edward Palmer and Henry Abelove, 'E. P. Thompson', in E. P. Thompson and Henry Abelove, et al. (eds.), *Visions of History* (Manchester: Manchester University Press, 1976), pp. 3–27.

Thompson, Sir H., *Modern Cremation: Its History and Practice* (London: Paul, Trench, Trübner, 1891).

Thompson, Sir Henry, *The Motor-Car: An Elementary Handbook on Its Nature Use and & Management* (London: F. Warne and Co., 1902).

Titmash, Belgrave [Charles Ebenezer Moyse], *Shakspere's Skull and Falstaff's Nose: A Fancy in Three Acts* (London: E. Stock, 1889).

A Treatise on Fevers (London: Seagood and Collins, 1788).

Tringham, Ruth and Annie Davis, 'Doing Sensory Archaeology: The Challenges', in Robin Skeates and Jo Day (eds.), *The Routledge Handbook of Sensory Archaeology* (London: Routledge, 2020), pp. 47–75.

Trollope, Anthony, *The Fixed Period* (London: William Blackford and Sons, 1882).

Tsing, Anna Lowenhaupt, *The Mushroom at the End of the World: On the Possibility of Life in Capitalist Ruins* (Oxford: Princeton University Press, 2015).

Tullett, William, 'Grease and Sweat: Race and Smell in Eighteenth-century English Culture', *Cultural and Social History*, 13:6 (2016), pp. 307–22.

Tullett, William, 'PastScent Bibliography', https://www.zotero.org/groups/4530561/pastscent/library [accessed 13/01/2022].

Tullett, William, 'Re-odorisation, Disease, and Emotion in Mid-nineteenth-century England', *The Historical Journal*, 62:3 (2019), pp. 765–88.

Tullett, William, *Smell in Eighteenth-century England: A Social Sense* (Oxford: Oxford University Press, 2019).

Tullett, William and Hannah McCann, 'Sensing the Pandemic: Revealing and Re-ordering the Senses', *The Senses and Society*, 17:2 (2022), pp. 170–84.

Turkel, William J., 'Intervention: Hacking History, from Analogue to Digital and Back Again', *Rethinking History*, 15:2 (2011), pp. 287–96.

Turner, James, *Philology: The Forgotten Origins of the Modern Humanities* (Oxford: Princeton University Press, 2014).

Uchacz, Tianna Helena, 'Reconstructing Early Modern Artisanal Epistemologies and an "Undisciplined" Mode of Inquiry', *Isis*, 111:3 (2020), pp. 606–13.

Wall, John N., 'Transforming the Object of Our Study: The Early Modern Sermon and the Virtual Paul's Cross Project', *Journal of Digital Humanities*, 3:1 (2014), http://journalofdigitalhumanities.org/3-1/transforming-the-object-of-our-study-by-john-n-wall/ [accessed 07/03/2022].

War Office, *Treatise on Ammunition* (London: HM Stationary Office, 1915).

Wauters, Wendy, 'Smelling Disease and Death in the Antwerp Church of Our Lady, c. 1450–1559', *Early Modern Low Countries*, 5:1 (2021), pp. 17–39.

Welch, Evelyn, 'Scented Buttons and Perfumed Gloves: Smelling Things in Renaissance Italy', in Bella Mirabella (ed.), *Ornamentalism: The Art of Renaissance Accessories* (Ann Arbor: University of Michigan Press, 2011), pp. 13–39.

Wicky, Érika, 'Perfumed Performances: The Reception of Olfactory Theatrical Devices from Fin-de-siecle to the Present Day', in Nele Wyants (ed.), *Media Archaeology and Intermedial Performance: Deep Time of the Theatre* (Cham: Palgrave Macmillan, 2019), pp. 129–43.

Williams, Morris J., 'Smells and Their Classification', *The Lancet*, 174:4502 (1909), pp. 1795–6.

Williams, Phillip, 'The Rosemary Theme in Romeo and Juliet', *Modern Language Notes*, 68:6 (1953), p. 402.

Wolter, Friedrich, 'Die Nebelkatastrophe Im Maastal Sudlich Von Luttich', *Klinische Wochenschrift*, 10:17 (1931), pp. 785–8.

Young, Alison, 'The Limits of the City: Atmospheres of Lockdown', *British Journal of Criminology* (2021), doi: 10.1093/bjc/azab001.

Zwaardemaker, Henrik, *Die Physiologie des Geruchs* (Leipzig: Wilhelm Engelmann, 1895).

Index

Acrid 15, 19, 24, 54, 112
Agency 33–4
Ahnfelt, Nils-Otto 73
Air 79
Alcohol 84, 111, 115
Ambergris 88
Ammonia viii, 24–5, 114
Amsterdam 104
Animals 25; death caused by pollution 24 (*see also* Civet Cat; Dogs; Goats; Horses; Molecular Commons; Musk Deer; Pigs); as prosthesis for human noses 29
Anosmia 7, 8, 16, 81, 114
Anthropocentrism 28, 70. *See also* Animals
Anthropology 1, 117
Antiquarianism 56
Archaeology 14, 15, 92
Archives 3, 10, 45, 57–8, 61–2, 66, 67, 69, 117; Air as 121 (*see also* Libraries; Osmothéque); Digitization of 8; Environment as 53, 68–9, 80–1; of sound 59; Odours as 3, 75, 92; of smell 47, 63–4, 70
Armstrong, Edward 55–6
Aromarama 97–9. *See also* Smell-o-vision
Articulation 15, 44, 95, 96
Atmo-orientalism 78. *See also* Racism
Attention 26–7, 34–5
Automobiles 35–8, 84; Air-fresheners in 21–3; as heritage 38; Smell of 20–1; Sound of 20

Babbage, Charles 121
Bacteriology 26, 82, 85
Balsam 4
Barthes, Roland 17
Battlefields 54. *See also*, War, Waterloo
Bees 31, 83
Beijing 51, 75
Benzoin viii, 108

Bitter almonds 24, 68, 114
Black Country 90
Bland, John Otway Percey 51
Bleach viii
Bloch, Marc 120. *See also* Annales
Bodies 3, 109; as archives 66; Blood 115 (*see also* Habit; Decay; Death); Flatulence 84; Permeability of 34; and reading 14; Rotting 101, 104 110–11, 111, 112; Space between 7; Sweat 84
Books viii, 57; Production of 18–19; Odour wheel of 63; Old smell of 20, 66, 85
Botany 50
Braudel, Fernard 107. *See also* Annales
Bread 98
Breath 7, 51, 84
Brussels 51

Cabbage 19, 93
Cadaverine 110. *See also* Death; Decay
Camera inodorata 100. *See also* Psychology
Camphor 96
Candles 7, 46; Beeswax 4; Tallow 101
Carbolic 85
Casimiro, Tânia Manuel 73
Catholicism 4
Cedarwood 97
Chemistry 49, 50
Chen, Anna 3
Chloride of Lime viii, 68, 85–6, 112
Cholera 69, 70
Churches 4, 102, 104–5
Cities 16, 19, 28–9, 37, 50, 80. *See also* Amsterdam; Beijing; Brussels; Cologne; Glasgow; Liverpool; London; Paris; St. Louis
Civet 46, 80, 91. *See also* Animals
Civet cat 46, 91. *See also* Civet
Civetone 91
Class 19, 58, 84, 89, 90

Climate change 10, 40
Coal 19, 31, 35, 39, 93, 103
Coffee 98, 101–2; grading 15; houses 84, 101
Coleridge, Samuel Taylor 49
Cologne, City of 49
Computers 67
Corbin, Alain 13
Cordite 112–13. *See also* Guns; Gunpowder
Covid-19 pandemic 6–9
Creosote 112
Cupere, Peter de 41

Damp 66
Death 87, 104, 109, 110–11; Cremation 86–7 (*see also* Animals; Bodies; Cadaverine; Decay)
Decay 16, 39, 77, 101, 104, 110, 111. *See also* Damp; Death; Mould; Putridity; Rust
Decolonization 44
Deodorization 86, 100, 101, 121; differential 19–20, 23, 32; narrative 50, 80; temporal structure of 83–8; writing as 17, 20 (*see also* Chloride of Lime; Disinfection)
Digital humanities 50, 52
Disease 26, 85. *See also* Cholera; Covid19-pandemic; Plague
Disinfectants 31, 84, 90, 96, 97, 101. *See also* Chloride of Lime
Distillation 45–6, 57. *See also* Extractive Imagination
Distribution of the sensible 27–8, 35, 44, 56. *See also* Attention
Dogs 28–9, 70–1, 83, 103; robotic 69
Durian fruit 89

Earp, J. R. 101
Environments 31, 35, 52; as affordances 4, 33, 53; as an archive 53, 68–9, 80–1; Institutional 85; Intermingling of bodies with 34; Pre- and post-historical 15; Pre-industrial 22; of reading 11; Urban 87; Utopian 22; (*see also* Climate Change; Homes; Laboratory; Oceans; Offices; Slums; Water)
Epistemicide 42–4

Evans, Joan 50–1
Extractive imagination 52, 59

Febvre, Lucien 120. *See also* Annales
Fish 18, 78
Flavour science 63
Fleay, Frederick Gard 50
Flowers 31. *See also* Lavender, Lilies, Rose; Gardeners
Food 26–7, 72–3, 95–6; Baking 76; Butchers 105; Cooking 16, 90, 91; Kitchens 86; Sweets 71
Ford 38
Freshness 25. *See also* Decay
Fuel 19, 86, 103. *See also* Coal; Gas; Petrol
Fumigation 69. *See also* Disinfection
Fungi 30
Furnivall, Frederick James 49
Future 21–3, 37, 81, 86; futurological fiction 86–8

Gamble, Eleanor Acheson McCulloch 100
Gardeners 2. *See also* Flowers
Garlic 61, 89, 114
Gas-warfare 113–14
Gas, works 67; Lighting 85; Masks 114–15; Warfare 109, 113–14
Ghettos 51
Glasgow 19, 68–9
Goats 61
Gramsci, Antonio 14
Grass 21–2, 98
Griffin, Alfred 111
Gumbrech, Hans Ulrich 72. *See also* Presence
Gunpowder 112. *See also* Cordite; Guns
Guns 43. *See also* Gunpowder; Cordite

Habit 16, 54, 65, 78, 121
Habituation 23–4, 32, 35 105
Hartmann, Sadakichi 97, 99
Hauntology 88. *See also* Time; Future
Hawkesworth, John 108
Hazoumé, Romuald 61
Hell 16, 78, 93, 102–3
Henning, Hans 101
Heritage 2
Heritage Science 8, 53, 63, 67; Techniques for capturing odours in 64

Historical distance 2, 42
History 121; Annales school of 107, 120; Anosmic nature of 8; Cultural 2; Experimental approaches to 6, 72, 117; of emotions 14, 53, 121; evolution as academic discipline 55–6; and temporality 42; and meaning 4, 72; Oral, 89–90
Holy water 102
Homes 20, 80
Horses 36, 110
Hungary water 95, 96
Hyperobjects 41

Incense viii, 4, 75, 97, 105, 108; Censors 5; Clocks 75–6
Indole 91
Industry; fulling 25; paper mills 18, 27; tanning 25
Interdisciplinarity 5, 63, 117–18
International Flavours and Fragrance 22–3, 64, 102–3
Intersubjectivity 63–4

James, Henry 1
Jeremijenko, Natalie 68
Jesuits 43, 103
Jünger, Ernst 114

Kant, Immanuel 45, 65
Kettler, Andrew 43

Laboratory 99
Lacey, Kate 59
Ladurie, Emmanuel Le Roy 56
Language 60–1, 62; alters olfactory perception 17; Binary language of 62; Historians prisoner of 13; Linguistic turn 9; Odours as a lingua-franca 28
Latour, Bruno 96
Laube, Hans 97
Lavender 4
Lawson, John 43
Leather 66, 67, 73, 114
Lemon 90, 91
Libraries 20, 57–8, 67; Odour bans in 58 (*see also* Archives)
Lilies 4

Liverpool 40
London 23–5, 31, 51; Bucklersbury 47, 48, 49; great stink of 40; underground 26

Majid, Asifa 62
Margolles, Teresa 41
Matches viii, 32
Materiality 3, 74; Architecture 3; Objects 3, 73–4, 80–1
Maurer, Edward 106
Maxim, Harim 113
McGee, Harold 3
McHugh, James 74
McNeile, H. C. 113
Medicines viii, 48, 71, 101, 117; Druggists 25, 48; Humoral 72–3, 95–6; Paracelsian 93
Memory 2, 35–6, 54, 77, 105; geographical exploration of 90
Micro-film 67
Molecular commons 29–31
Molecules 92, 94, 121; volatile organic compounds 3, 91
Monelli, Paolo 111
Mould 56
Moyse, Charles Ebenezer 47, 117
Murphey, Grace
Muscone 91
Museums 44, 61, 102–3, 109, 110
Musk 46, 80
Musk deer 46

Narrative 11, 75; Smell as a medium for staging 94
Natural philosophy 46
Newstead, Sarah 73
Nissan 22
Nose 10; becoming a 15; Dead Man's 54; Holding the 16; Perfumers' 62; Researchers' 14; Selectivity of 70; Sensitivity of 24, 49, 70, 98
Novels 1

Oceans 16
Odeuropa ix, 5–6
Odour of sanctity 108
Odours; as archives 3, 15; Classification of 99–101, 106; Durability of 46; Gamut of 106 (*see also* Smell; Nose); implicit

in texts 16; Medicinal power of 48; Prophylactic power of 25, 80, 96; and multispecies communication 28–30; Regulation of 15, 52, 63–4, 73, 86; as weapon 26
Offices 20
Oken, Lorenz 43
Olfactorium 100. *See also* Psychology
Olfactory art 41, 61, 109
Olfactory facsimiles 35, 39
Onion 40
Osmothèque 63–4
Ozone 86

Pacific 108–9
Paint 90, 91
Paradise 108–9
Paraffin oil 18
Paris 50, 51, 58
Parosmia 7–8
Pedagogy 72–3
Perfumery 15, 52, 60, 66, 73, 85, 90, 95, 97, 109; Fixatives in 46, 80, 109; Heritage of 48; Perfume structures 106–7; Perfumed gloves 91; Perfumed wigs 101; Training in 16; use of by men 47 (*see also* Synthetic odours)
Petrol 21, 27, 73
Phantosmia 8
Philology 49
Piesse, Septimus 106
Pigs 30, 70
Pine 96, 97
Pinksky, Michael 41
Plague 25, 85, 96, 103
Plastic 73
Poetry 45, 76, 111
Poland 51
Policymakers 40, 44
Pollution 16, 20, 26, 40, 79, 83, 93; buried waste 68–9; disappearance of 22–3 (*see also* Automobiles; Coal; Industry; Smog); as positive smell 89; as smell of 'success' 27
Pomander 80, 103–4, 109
Pot-pourri 65
Poucher, William 106
Presence 6, 33, 72; Presentification 94–5
Proust, Marcel 35–6, 77, 121

Psychology 99–101
Public engagement 13
Public history 2
Púcaros 74
Putrescine 110. *See also* Death; Decay
Putridity 61, 103. *See also* Putrescine

Racism 43, 58, 78, 89. *See also* Atmoorientalism; Epistemicide; Slavery
Ramazzini, Bernadino 117
Ranke, Leopold von 55
Re-odorization 39, 53, 84. *See also* Deodorization
Reade, Walter 97
Reconstruction 16, 54, 102–4; as tool for atmospheric re-sensitization 41–2
Reformation 82
Religion 4, 74, 108, 117. *See also* Catholicism; Churches; Hell; Holy water; Incense; Jesuits; Odour of Sanctity; Paradise; Reformation; Rosaries
Ricci, Matteo 75
Rimmel, Eugene 48
Robinson, James Harvey 50
Roinard, Paul-Napoléon 97
Root beer viii, 71
Rosaries 102, 103
Rose 2
Rosemary viii, 4, 85, 95–6
Rotten-eggs 15
Rubber 38, 93, 114
Rushes 105
Rust 115

Saffron viii, 73
Sanitation 2; Night-soil 48; Progressive narratives of 50–1, 76 (*see also* Waste); Sanitarians 2, 52, 101; Sewage 39, 40
Santee 43
Sassoon, Siegfried 112
Schaffner, Martin 102–3
Scott, Walter 110–11
Seeley, John Robert 55
Selfhood 77
Senses; Hierarchies of 42–3, 74; Separation of 100 (*see also* Attention; Smell; Sound; Taste; Touch; Vision)
Sensory Studies 1; Waves of 9

Shakespeare, William 45, 47, 49, 78–9, 117
Shapin, Steven 63
Shiel, M. P. 114
Shoe polish 73
Silage 114
Skatole 91
Slavery 61. *See also* Racism
Sloterdijk, Peter 114
Slums 86, 87, 101
Smell-o-vision 61, 97–9
Smell-walking 15, 66
Smell; Absence of 33; against the grain 20; Definition of 91 (*see also* Odour; Nose); Desensitization to 11, 41; Ephemerality of 45–6, 65; as an intellectual tool 90–1; Olfactory-visual litany 46, 62; Monumentality of 54; as narrative trip-wire 89; Palimpsestic nature of 78–9, 81; in the past 1–2, 5; and the past 1, 2, 5; of the past 1, 3, 5; produced by change 10; and reality effect 8
Smelling salts viii
Smellscapes 1, 91, 102, 105; Everyday awareness of 10, 11; Background and foreground of 105; Mapping of 52–3, 79, 107–8
Smog 23, 32
Smoke viii
Sodium hyposulphite 114
Song of Songs 97
Sound 20; Audio-visual litany 46; Hearing 56; Music paired with smell 97, 106; Noise 27; of progress 27; Phonographic imagination 59–60; Silence 24; Soundscapes 52
Sousa Santos, Boaventura de 42
Space 3
Stanley, William 87
Stasi 70
St. Louis 32
Stubbes, Phillip 80
Sulphur 19, 69, 78–9, 88, 92–3, 103, 108; Hydrogen sulphide 15, 16, 57, 69, 111; Sulphur dioxide 15, 16, 24, 31, 32
Synthetic odours 23, 26, 39, 60, 97

Taste 61
Tennant, Charles 68

Theatres 4–5, 53, 78–9, 97, 98, 99
Thompson, Edward Palmer 56
Thresholds 11
Time 75–6, 81; Biblical 108 (*see also* Future); Blurring of 93; Duration of odours 105; Linear conception of 81–2, 93; longue durée 107; in perfumery 106–7, 109; Seasonal 76; Smell of 76, 77
Ting, Anna Lowenhaut 30
Tobacco 4, 66, 101; Smoking bans 84; Snuff 111; Tobacconists 25
Toolas, Sissel 64
Touch 102, 104, 120
Transduction 8, 64–5
Trauma 114
Travel 11, 108
Trollope, Anthony 87
Truffle oil viii
Truffles viii, 30, 56

Urine viii, 18, 114

Vanilla 109
Ventilation 57, 66, 86
Vinegar 67, 69
Vision 44; Influence of visual media on smell-media 98–9; interaction with smell 74; Ocularcentrism 9, 58–9, 72
Volcanoes 16, 93

Waldie, Charlotte 110
War 82, 109–15. *See also,* Battlefields, Cordite, Death, Gas-warfare, Gunpowder, Waterloo
Waste 109; Faecal odour 91 (*see also* Pollution; Sanitation); Human 85–6; Waste-water, Plumbing 86
Water 68, 74, 85, 90, 91, 101, 108; Stagnant 108
Waterloo 54, 110
Widnes 79
Williams, Morris J. 101
Wine-tasting 15
Wintergreen 71

Yi, Anika 41

Zwaademaker, Henrik 100

www.ingramcontent.com/pod-product-compliance
Lightning Source LLC
Chambersburg PA
CBHW061842300426
44115CB00013B/2483